ROMAN RHETORIC

ROMAN RHETORIC
REVOLUTION AND THE GREEK INFLUENCE

RICHARD LEO ENOS
Carnegie Mellon University

WAVELAND
PRESS, INC.
Prospect Heights, Illinois

Consulting Editor
Robert E. Denton, Jr.

For information about this book, write or call:

Waveland Press, Inc.
P.O. Box 400
Prospect Heights, Illinois 60070
(708) 634-0081

Cover Illustration: Figure 7, *Ancient Portraits from the Athenian Agora.* Courtesy of the American School of Classical Studies at Athens.

ISBN 0-88133-830-3

Printed in the United States of America

7 6 5 4 3 2 1

In memory of
my Great Aunt Giovanna
and my Grandmother Catterina

*In spiritu humilitatis, et in animo contrito suscipiamur a te,
Domine: et sic fiat sacrificium nostrum in conspectu tuo
hodie, ut placeat tibi, Domine Deus.*

Acknowledgments

My interest in ancient Rome and in rhetoric began (and re-began) at different times in my life. As a child, the stories of my ancestors' land and our heritage gave me pride and self-esteem. As a college student my first professor of classical rhetoric, Hal Barrett, inspired a love of rhetoric. In 1972 I was able to study in Italy through the programs offered by the Vergilian Society. That experience brought together and made real both the academic subjects of Roman Studies and rhetoric as well as a personal heritage and history. The study of Roman rhetoric became, for me, a study of not only the subject I love but the people I came to consider my own. Similarly, my experiences as a student of the American School of Classical Studies at Athens nurtured my strong feelings for the study of Greek rhetoric. As I continued to study both Greek and Roman rhetoric—an inquiry which was then done in very clear and separate ways—I began to note similarities and relationships not emphasized in my education. Over the years I felt that emphasizing these social and cultural interactions between Greek and Roman rhetoric would provide a better understanding of classical rhetoric than currently exists. To be able to offer readers insights into Greek and Roman rhetoric is a synthesis of education, feelings and desires that have been taking shape for many years.

Of particular value in this project is the availability of recent epigraphical evidence which extends our knowledge beyond extant, conventional literary sources. This new archaeological material is valuable in almost every period examined in this work. The early efforts of Greek colonization in the West, the nature and extent of Roman patronage of Greek literary and rhetorical arts, and the impact of rhetorical deliberation are all enhanced by our study of this new evidence. The research and analysis of these inscriptions was made possible through the support of the National Endowment for the Humanities and the cooperation of the Greek Ministry of Culture and The American School of Classical Studies at Athens.

The maps, photographs, and drawings that appear in this volume are the result of the cooperation of many individuals and institutions. Appreciation is extended to George Allen & Unwin, now HarperCollins Publishers Limited of Great Britain, for permission to reproduce the maps of Sicily and Southern Italy (p. 5) from A. G. Woodhead's *The Greeks in the West*. Lynda Ballinger of HarperCollins was most helpful. The American Classical League was kind enough to grant permission to reproduce the figure of the Roman Forum. Dr. Marian H. McAllister, Editor of Publications for the American School of Classical Studies at Athens, was instrumental in helping to secure permission to reproduce photographs and drawings that appear in various publications of the ASCS. Mrs. Jan Jordan, Secretary for the Agora Excavations of the ASCS, was likewise instrumental in helping to secure permission to reproduce archaeological illustrations. Only those who have done such tasks realize how valuable such cooperation and consideration can be in the preparation of a volume.

Students are influenced by their professors in at least two ways. The first is direct and obvious: the imparting of the substance of the discipline. The second way is indirect and less obvious: the disposition, approach and zeal by which that substance is imparted. After nearly twenty-five years of teaching I still have difficultly determining which is more important. I suppose that the answer is both, for I certainly benefited from scholars who excelled in these two dimensions. For those personal experiences I wish to thank J. Jeffery Auer, Robert Gray Gunderson, Raymond Smith, Harry Caplan, Everett Lee Hunt, and Wilbur Samuel Howell. If by no other source than personal experience, I am convinced that the Romans were accurate in stressing the value of learning by studying excellent models.

Lastly, I wish to thank the Banchio family for preserving and nurturing a love of heritage and the three decades of students who unceasingly rekindle enthusiasm with their eagerness to learn. I also wish to thank the Vergilian Society for the experience of studying in Italy that forever shaped my education and interest in Roman rhetoric. I also wish to thank Liese Leff for her many valuable suggestions on grammar and style; her recommendations on correctness and clarity have shaped both my expression and my appreciation for writing well. I wish to close this section by acknowledging the unfailing support of my friends at Waveland Press and Carol and Neil Rowe in particular. Their expertise and attitude are what all authors hope for in publishers.

RLE
Pittsburgh, PA

Preface

Teachers of classical rhetoric too often succumb to the temptation of making a leap from fifth and fourth century B.C. Athens into first century B.C. Rome with only token references to Hellenistic and pre-Ciceronian Roman rhetorical theory—and even fewer comments about the social and cultural forces that shaped the transmission and reception of rhetoric. This shallow to nonexistent treatment of three hundred years of history results less from the failure of the instructor to prepare the syllabus thoroughly than from the lack of comprehensive scholarship by researchers of classical rhetoric. Lacking adequate information about this transition, the introduction to Roman rhetoric offers little explanation about its contexts or its relationship with Greek rhetoric. Learning how Romans were exposed to Greek rhetoric and their initial attitudes toward it helps greatly to explain how Greek rhetoric was received and the impact it had on those Romans who fashioned their own rhetoric. Although we know somewhat more about how Romans later supported and sustained Greek rhetoric, our knowledge is limited to influential patrons. The purpose of this book is to help erase the void between Greek and Roman rhetoric by providing a context so that rhetorical theory and practice in ancient Rome can be better understood.

At the time when some of Rome's most important orations were being delivered, at the time when some of the most important treatises on Roman rhetoric were being composed, and at a time when some of her greatest literature was being written, Rome was in turmoil. Decades of civil war, violent political clashes, and proscription death lists were the result of opportunistic and ambitious dynasts attempting to seize power. Socially, the gains brought about by successful military campaigns extended Rome's Empire, increased armies and nurtured the rise of a merchant-oriented middle class intent on seizing commercial opportunities. Such sweeping changes cut across every aspect of Roman society. Captivated by the rise and fall of political institutions and the clash of mighty armies, we are tempted to overlook other, less evident forces at work. This volume is an effort to demonstrate the important role that rhetoric played in the transformations of Roman society from Republic to Empire. Through an examination of this important period, we will better understand rhetoric at work, a force we now understand only dimly. For students of the history of rhetoric, such an understanding is essential, for rhetorical theory devoid of context is not only incomplete but insensitive to the elements that shaped it.

The study of Roman history during this tumultuous period and the study of Roman rhetoric have persisted in an estranged, mutually limiting autonomy. Social and political forces helped shape the unique features of Roman rhetoric, particularly the modification of the Greek rhetoric from which it so clearly drew. Conversely, rhetoric contributed to social and political change. A work which integrates the endemic relationship between Roman history and the history of rhetoric at Rome will provide a more complete and sensitive accounting than exclusively independent renderings. This volume thus serves the same function as its earlier companion volume, *Greek Rhetoric Before Aristotle*—situating rhetoric within its cultural context.

In the final section of the Preface, I would like to underscore the last point and, in doing so, the scope and intent of this work. I will first commit the cardinal sin of authorship and describe the nature of this book by explaining what it does *not* do. This is not a book about how Greek rhetoric grew and evolved as a discipline unto itself within the historical periods of the Roman Republic and Empire. That is, it is not a volume about the evolution of the later Greek enlightenment of classical rhetoric called the Second Sophistic, although the impact of that phenomenon on Roman rhetoric will be discussed. Similarly, the dominant strains of Greek rhetoric that existed in the East during the later Roman Republic and early Empire, such as Asianism and Atticism, are discussed only when they bear directly on Roman views. Important rhetorical concepts, such as Greek *stasis* and its Latin equivalents *constitutio* and *status*, are discussed only by their limited use in Roman decla-mation and not by what Romans such as Cicero had to say in specific theoretical works. The same general approach is applied to prominent Greek thinkers of rhetoric and philosophy, who had much to say about theory and criticism but do not fit centrally with the explanation of rhetoric as a force in Roman society and culture beyond selected intellectual circles.

What then does this work treat and what contribution does it hope to make to its readers? All of the important topics of Greek rhetoric mentioned in the preceding paragraph are normally, and rightly, discussed as topics *within* the history of rhetoric itself, that is, the scholarly accounting of theoretical and critical contributions that mark the discipline. This volume emphasizes the social and cultural environment within which those activities took place in order to provide a better understanding of their context. This volume's task is to help readers "situate" rhetoric within Roman society during a very important period in her history—a period of enormous transition. Rhetoric was recognized by Romans as a source of power and used in a variety of ways ranging from political control to intellectual refinement. Understanding the Roman interest in rhetoric as a source for oral argument, for example, helps to explain its role in legal training and the courts during the Republic. Rhetoric as a subject that supplied the training and intellectual material for wisdom and eloquence helps to explain the Roman patronage of Greek sophists that nurtured the Second Sophistic. Readers will find the bibliography a welcome source for further study of the specific concepts, issues, individuals and theories of Greek rhetoric. The text of this book should help prepare them not only for that reading but, of course, to understand the particular characterizations, adaptations and departures that Romans made in fashioning their own rhetoric.

George Kennedy closed the final chapter of his 1963 volume, *The Art of Persuasion in Greece*, with the following remark:

> By the first century it was already evident that rhetorical studies were as much at home in Rome as in Athens and that conditions of Roman oratory, the attitudes of Roman students, and the problems of adapting Greek rhetoric to the Latin language were the most potent factors in contemporary rhetoric. Thus the limit of this book has been reached (336).

Kennedy's 1972 volume, *The Art of Rhetoric in the Roman World*, does an excellent job of discussing later sophists and Greek rhetoricians of the Empire. His 1983 volume, *Greek Rhetoric Under Christian Emperors*, does a masterful job of following the internal development of the subject in the later Empire. None of these volumes concentrate on the social and cultural "factors" that conditioned their acceptance into the Roman world. This volume seeks to provide a bridge between Greek and Roman rhetoric by explaining those forces which influenced, and were influenced by, rhetoric in this period of social and intellectual revolution.

Contents

chapter 1

Forces Shaping the Transition from Greek to Roman Rhetoric

Most of our efforts to understand classical rhetoric center on shaping or sharpening our knowledge through a prominent individual, treatise or concept. While theoretically acknowledging that rhetoric is best understood within its context, we persist in isolating and abstracting rhetorical theory in practice—sacrificing (or ignoring) *in situ* conditions for the precision of analysis in a vacuum. This chapter offers an explanation of the political and social forces that motivated Athens to promote rhetoric not only at home but in colonies and among allies in Sicily and southern Italy. Athenian influence in the West not only created strong political ties with kindred cities but fostered the study of arts such as rhetoric. The introduction of rhetoric in Rome was not so much the consequence of direct contact by Romans traveling to Athens but rather a prolonged process of exposure to schools of rhetoric from the Greek colonies in Sicily and southern Italy.

Athenian Imperialism in the West and Its Impact on Greek and Roman Rhetoric

Around 444 B.C.E. Pericles sought to establish a colony at Thurii. The exact political motivation behind this is in doubt, but it was certainly part of Athenian imperialism (Edward Schiappa, 1991:179).

Although rhetoric probably had its formal beginnings in Sicily (Enos 1993), it was Athenian colonization that helped to nurture and perpetuate the study of rhetoric in both Sicily and southern Italy. Rhetoric was introduced to Rome principally through Greek colonies rather than directly from the intellectual center of Athens. This chapter offers an explanation of Athenian political motivation in the West, the role that rhetoric played in the process, the efforts of sophists to act as agents for democratic imperialism, and its subsequent impact on Greek and Roman rhetoric.

The awareness of a relationship between facile expression and democracy is long-standing; what is not well established are the reasons for such attachments. What is the nature and status of that association of rhetoric and democracy? Was it coincidental, co-existent and complementary, or was it causal? That is, did the study of rhetoric in some way promote democracy or (in reverse) did the institution of democracy induce rhetoric? The safe answer is that many such relationships—causal, complementary, co-existent and even coincidental—did exist. We will explore evidence that there was a dimension of the relationship between rhetoric and democracy which was conscious, planned, and tactical.

Athenian Democracy and the *Dunamis* of Rhetoric

A first step to a fuller understanding of the relationship between rhetoric and democracy is to reconsider long-standing presumptions about the role of sophists. Scholarship has often stressed the association of sophists and Athenian democracy by limiting the relationship to political philosophy and intellectual curiosity. While it is true that democracy was intellectually compatible with many sophists (Poulakos 1990; Schiappa 1990), that ideological harmony alone does not explain its subsequent impact. Athenian imperialism, particularly in the West, offers one rationale.

Ancient authors had helpful observations about the relationship of rhetoric and democracy. Readers of Plato's *Gorgias* often focus on the comments of Socrates, Gorgias and Polus in order to discern the issues in the debate over the merits of rhetoric. In the background of this dialogue is Callicles, the Athenian democrat who represents the practical, pragmatic concerns of his community (e.g. 482C–486D; 490A). For most of us, Callicles has only a minor role in the dialogue; he is, after all, the only fictitious character in Plato's composition. In another sense, however, Callicles is the most real, for Callicles is the audience who will evaluate the respective and comparative views on rhetoric articulated by Socrates, Gorgias and Polus—and ultimately judge which perspective best serves Athenian democracy. Callicles' notion of rhetoric in the "service" of democracy best characterizes the information in this chapter.

Plato's *Gorgias* (e.g. 452E; 456A; 468E) and Aristotle's *Rhetoric* (e.g. 1359b) both address the *dunamis* or power of rhetoric. These discussions, however, treat the power of rhetoric in terms of its ability to enhance individual expression. Rhetoric was a source of power in a democracy because one's ability in expression could direct civic affairs by securing action through persuasion. The Roman rhetorician, Quintilian, saw *dunamis* as the power (*vim*) of persuasion and credited Isocrates with first recognizing this faculty in rhetoric (2. 15. 3–4). Rhetoric in an Athenian democracy had another dimension of *dunamis*: its utility in Athenian imperialism. The agents for rhetoric, at home and abroad, were the sophists. While it is true that sophists such as Gorgias and Polus had no real power in Athens, they were recognized by wily democrats as a tool for promoting Athenian interests. Aristotle, at least on this point, understood the mutual attraction that existed between sophists and democrats, for in his *Ethica Nicomachea* he made it apparent that he understood well the sophists' claim to teach political knowledge and viewed politics and rhetoric as an inherent relationship (1180b30–1181a17; Wilcox 1992: 154).

The close association of rhetoric and democracy was suspected even by opponents of the latter. After Athens lost to Sparta in the Peloponnesian War, the Spartans replaced democracy in Athens with the oligarchical rule of the Thirty Tyrants, that is, thirty conservative Athenians "acceptable" to the Spartans. The Spartans were no supporters of democracy and, as Quintilian records, banished the study of rhetoric in their own city (2. 16. 4). The rule of the Thirty Tyrants was short, for democracy was reinstated when Spartan influence diminished. In a telling move, the Thirty Tyrants successfully passed a law forbidding instruction in rhetoric by the sophists (Xenophon, *Memorabilia* 1. 2. 31). Stanley Wilcox's (1942: 155) observation on this act is insightful, for he argued that the oligarchs shrewdly discerned that trained rhetors meant individuals "capable of arousing the people, and a democratic party organized and united by effective speakers might mean the end of their oligarchical power." Recognizing rhetoric as a source of power, as "the life-blood of democracy," Wilcox noted, the oligarchs "shut off the flow at the source, the schools of rhetoric" (155).

Sophists were not uniformly pro-democratic (Schiappa 1991:

174, n. 52), but it is not difficult to see why many sophists—particularly those most prominent in rhetoric—were sympathetic to democracy. While obvious, it is important to state that politicians were active participants in the managing of Athenian democracy. The body of politicians came from the hoplite or middle/upper-middle class of propertied Athenians. These politicians, far outnumbering both the poorer and aristocratic citizen classes, were active in municipal administration as well as foreign affairs. In fact, epigraphical evidence indicates that many of these politicians served as ambassadors (Perlman 1963: 328, 335–36). In a democratic society where facile expression was a source of power, these newly rich politicians were a primary and eager audience for the rhetorical instruction of "political excellence" offered by sophists (Adkins 1973). In short, Athenian-style democracy was a political system that inherently encouraged rhetoric as a source of power for ambitious middle-class politicians. The large numbers and financial resources of these politicians offered sufficient incentive for sophists to be sympathetic to Athenian democracy at home and abroad.

Early Greek Colonization in the West and Athenian Thalassocracy

Although Sicily and southern Italy were long recognized as valuable for colonization and trade, early Athenian involvement was comparatively late and modest. The Chalcidians from Euboea are reported by Thucydides (6. 3, 4) as being the first to actively colonize in Sicily when they founded Naxos and later, using Naxos as a base, were instrumental in establishing Leontini and Catana. Syracuse was founded a year after Naxos by the Corinthians, whose influence increased as Syracuse continued to grow in prominence. Many Greek sites were founded by replacing or absorbing native inhabitants of Sicily. Megara established Megara Hyblaea and Selinus after considerable warfare with native dwellers and competing Greek colonies. Even far-distant islands such as Crete and Rhodes established colonies in the West, including Gela and later Acragas. Early activity of colonization similar to Sicily also took place in southern Italy, which offered fertile, corn-producing land so attractive to colonists that the southern Italian plains became densely populated with Greek villages (Dunbabin 1948/1989: 23, 146). The Euboeans were principally responsible for establishing Greek sites in Italy, such as Rhegium but, as Dunbabin notes, "the Southern Italian colonies were founded for

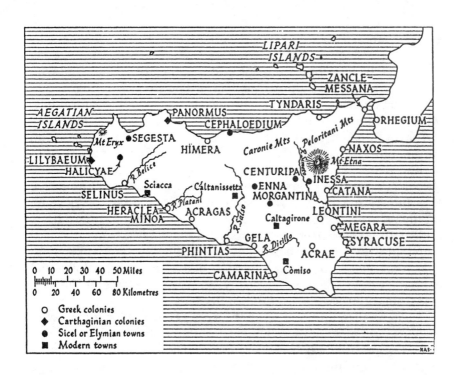

Map 1. Sicily

○	Greek colonies
◆	Carthaginian colonies
●	Sicel or Elymian towns
■	Modern towns

LIPARI ISLANDS

ZANCLE-MESSANA

AEGATIAN ISLANDS — PANORMUS — TYNDARIS — RHEGIUM

CEPHALOEDIUM

Mt Eryx ● SEGESTA — Caronie Mts — Peloritani Mts — NAXOS

LILYBAEUM — HIMERA — Mt Etna

HALICYAE — R.Belice — CENTURIPA — INESSA — CATANA

Sciacca — Caltanissetta — ENNA — MORGANTINA

SELINUS — R.Platani — ACRAGAS — Caltagirone — LEONTINI

HERACLEA-MINOA — R.Salso — MEGARA

GELA — R.Dirillo — SYRACUSE

PHINTIAS — ACRAE

CAMARINA — Còmiso

0 10 20 30 40 50 Miles
0 20 40 60 80 Kilometres

Map 2. Southern Italy

BARIUM

NEAPOLIS

CUMAE — POMPEII — R.Bradano — Matera — BRUNDISIUM

ISCHIA — SALERNUM — POTENTIA

R.Sele — R.Basento — TARAS — LAECAE

POSIDONIA (PAESTUM) — METAPONTUM

ELEA

PYXUS

TYRRHENIAN SEA — Castrovillari

SYBARIS-THURII

Belvedere Marittima — R.Crati — R.Trionto — Cirò

CONSENTIA — R.Neto — CROTON

Sila — IONIAN SEA

Catanzaro

LIPARI ISLANDS — HIPPONIUM — CAULONIA

LIPARI — R.Allaro

LOCRI

ZANCLE-MESSANA — RHEGIUM

Melito — C.Spartivento

0 10 20 30 40 50 Miles
0 20 40 60 80 Kilometres

○	Cities of Greek foundation
■	Cities of ancient but non-Greek foundation
●	Modern towns

the most part by people from both sides of the Corinthian Gulf who were not themselves commercial'' (23). The sites of southern Italy were particularly attractive locations for intellectual communities, with prominent thinkers often coming from as far as Ionia. Pythagoras came from Samos to establish his school at Croton (Dunbabin 1948/1989: 361); Parmenides and Zeno also settled in southern Italy at Elea. Established colonies, such as Syracuse, themselves became colonists and founded such cities as Camarina. It is interesting to note that both Syracuse and Croton became highly regarded as intellectual centers in Sicily and southern Italy, and both experienced attempts at replacing aristocratic and oligarchical systems with democracies (Dunbabin 1948/1989: 371). The relationship between sophists, democracy and intellectual centers would become critically important elements in the transmission of Greek rhetoric to Rome.

These sites and many others were colonized for a variety of reasons, and most of these reasons remain at the level of specula- tion. The obvious advantages of colonization include the need to repopulate because of limited resources of founding sites, the advantages of trade, strong agricultural bases and strategic locations for war. It is likely that all are reasonable explanations to warrant the activity in the West. Thucydides' meticulous ac- counting of early Greek colonization in the West makes Athens conspicuous by her absence. Athenian efforts at control, however, were no less constrained by the lack of early colonization, and rhetoric was an important tool to advance her imperial plans in the West.

Athens' tumultuous history explains her late efforts at colonization. As a fortification, the Acropolis of Athens dates back to the Bronze Age. As with many other Greek cities, Athens was ruled by monarchy and later by an aristocracy. Movements toward democracy began in Athens as early as the sixth century B.C. when Solon's liberation of debt-slaves in 594 B.C. and other fiscal reforms began to shift economic power away from the aristocracy. For much of the sixth century B.C. Athens was ruled by tyrants, and during this period the arts and trade flourished. The continuing struggle for power between the aristocracy and the emerging democracy, however, compelled Athens to devote much of her attention and effort to internal conflicts and not to take advantage of colonization as did many of her more stable sister cities. The overthrow of the final tyrant, Hippias, in 510 B.C. and the reforms directed by Cleisthenes signaled the establishment of a true democracy. Athens' famous victories over the Persian Empire at Marathon (490 B.C.)

and at Salamis (480/479 B.C.) not only solidified the democracy but opened the way to an active foreign policy, particularly in the West.

Although Athens' late entry in establishing claims of territory in the West somewhat limited the possibilities of colonization, her rise to power in the fifth century B.C. and strong imperialistic drive resulted in active campaigns to establish hegemony in the West. Athens sought to establish strong allies by promoting Western democracies, as well as securing allegiance with oligarchies. The Athenian strategy to secure domination in the West was to break old allegiances between founding colonies and their mother cities. One way that Athens sought to make alliances in the West was through claims of kinship. This strategy had, at best, limited success. Many of these colonies were Dorians or Dorians through kinship (Thucydides 6. 6) and thus viewed themselves as different from the Athenians. Other, non-Dorian cities had colonized in the West, and Athens sought to establish authority through claiming kinship with her more closely related Euboean-descended sites such as Naxos, Catana and Leontini. On the basis of this strained interpretation of kinship, Athens entered into alliances that provided the rationale (and pretext) warranting political involvement (Thucydides 6. 50; Diodorus Siculus 12. 53–54). "To admit to the truest motive," wrote Thucydides, " [the Athenians] wanted to rule the whole area, but at the same time they wished to appear to be coming to the rescue of their kinfolk and old allies" (6. 6).

In addition to promoting alliances through treaties, Athens eventually pursued colonization. Athens' late and limited efforts at colonization resulted in the establishment of Thurii and Neapolis (Naples) in southern Italy (Plutarch, *Pericles* 11. 5; Sealey 1976: 309; Graham 1983:36). Pro-Athenian sophists played important roles in the growth of Thurii, a city that gained a reputation as an intellectual center through such naturalized citizens as Herodotus and Polus. Herodotus and Protagoras, for example, were both close supporters of Pericles and his democratic views. Edward Schiappa underscores Protagoras' important task of "creating the constitution or laws" of Thurii (179). That Pericles selected a non-Athenian sophist for the task is important because it demonstrates the key role sophists played in spreading Athenian concepts and Athenian recognition for that ability. Other, less eminent sophists such as Euthydemus and Dionysodorus also resided at Thurii for several years (Plato, *Euthydemus* 217 B.C.) and helped to establish the city as an important intellectual center and a recognized site for the study of rhetoric. Athenian efforts to secure imperial gains in this late period were so aggressive that they even sought to establish cleruchies, or the settlement of Athenian citizens abroad (Graham 1983:167). Plutarch lists Thurii as one of Athens' cleruchies (*Pericles* 1. 5; Graham 1983:169, 199). Athenian efforts at Thurii were democratic and imperialistic (Ehrenberg). That is, Athenians believed that expanding their empire was possible by developing and supporting allies who were sympathetic to democracy. The participation of sophists in securing and maintaining these ties was extremely important and, as we shall see, often utilized. Thurii was not an exception but a paradigm of Athens' expansionist ends and the role that sophists played. These activities and their consequences are critical to understanding the impact on Greek and Roman rhetoric in the West.

Athenians used two instruments to promote democracy in the West. First, as mentioned above, Athens actively secured agreement with a number of western sites such as Leontini and Rhegium through formal alliances and treaties, as well as active participation in the foundation of such cities as Neapolis (Naples) and Thurii (Graham 1983: 36). Ample literary evidence testifies to the existence of these agreements, such as Thucydides' account of the Athenian alliance with Corcyra (1. 44–55). In addition to literary references, fragments of actual treaties have survived. Two extant epigraphical sources are particularly important. The first is a treaty between Athens and Leontini that is now housed at the Epigraphical Museum at Athens (*Inscriptiones Graecae* 1 [2]. 52; Enos 1992). The second (similar) treaty is between Athens and Rhegium in Southern Italy and is now stored at the British Museum (*Inscriptiones Graecae* 1. [2]. 51). These inscriptions are two illustrations of Athenian efforts to promote democracy and secure alliances as the sort of base that Thucydides described Athens making with Chalkidian cities (3. 86; Freeman 616–26). In short, such treaties provide both the legitimation for Athens to enter into affairs in the West to "protect" her allies and the opportunity to expand in the West by conquering opposing cities.

A synthesis of literary and epigraphical sources confirms the second instrument to promote democracy mentioned above: Athenians entrusted sophists with the responsibility of securing alliances (Diodorus Siculus 12. 53). Treatises were executed through elder statesmen, or *presbyters*. These elders functioned as ambassadors who established treaty arrangements with Athens. Presbyters attended meetings in the ekklesia at Athens where the treaties of alliance were deliberated (Thucydides 6. 6) and gave formal speeches. These presbyters' speeches appear to be common and may prompt us to reexamine Cecil W. Wooten's claim that "the ambassador's speech does not seem to have developed as a distinct genre until the Hellenistic period [323–30 B.C.]" (209). Gorgias of Leontini, for example, was a presbyter when he went to Athens to establish treaty arrangements with his city in 427 B.C. as was Tisias of Syracuse (Diodorus Siculus 12. 53; Roberts 1904). The normal arrangement was to have the merits and particulars of the alliance debated in public and then inscribed on a marble stele.

It is clear that sophists did play a role in such negotiations and consistently spoke in favor of Athenian alliances with their Western cities. For those interested in the role of rhetoric, one of the most important observations that can be made of this phenomenon is the part that other prominent sophists played. Almost every prominent sophist and logographer known to us in this period exhibits some active political role in promoting Athenian-based democracy or in establishing strong ties with Athens. Empedocles, reputed to be the founder of rhetoric, was active in establishing democracy in Acragas by helping to emancipate Acragas from Emmenid tyranny (Woodhead 158). Gorgias is well known to us for his active role in promoting democracy in Leontini (Enos 1992), as well as Polus of Agrigentum, who is believed to have established a school of rhetoric in the Athenian colony of Thurii. Similarly, Corax and Lysias were other Western Greeks involved in democratic activities and, in Lysias' case in particular, with established ties with Athens (Enos 1993: 68). Some sophists served as presbyters, others doubtlessly as sycophants, but all were active supporters of democracy in the West. The consistency of the involvement of prominent sophists between their native and naturalized cities and Athens goes beyond the coincidental. Sophists served the causes of Athenian democracy well, not only by establishing the study of rhetoric as a source of power within democracies but also by using their suasive skills to extend and maintain democracies and political alliances with Athens in the West.

The value of sophists to Athenian imperialism helps to explain the sustained support they enjoyed beyond the altruistic merits of artistic patronage and the lofty goals of Plato's intellectual *paideia*. Plato's views on rhetoric were judged on the standards of intellectual integrity and claims of knowledge. Yet, it is obvious that democrats, who are symbolized by the dialogue character Callicles, saw in sophistic rhetoric a tool for democracy that was not at all on Plato's agenda: an agent for imperialism and a means for securing hegemony. Clearly rhetoric thrives in democracies, where normative and regulative functions of law, politics and ceremonial functions are mediated and judged through effective expression to and by a participating citizenry. To this extent the relationship of sophistic rhetoric and democracy was mutually beneficial. This symbiotic relationship promoted and used sophistic rhetoric as a way of maintaining the fragile democracies of the West and their alliances with Athens. The promoting of democracies in the West and the role sophists played in such cities have yet another consequence, one much further reaching than their initial impact in the fifth century B.C.

Athens built her base of power in the West through subject allies, using sophists and rhetoric as tools for democratic security and expansion. In 427 B.C., for example, Gorgias of Leontini went to Athens as a presbyter from Leontini to plea for Athens against Syracuse (Enos 1992). Using sophists as spokespersons for an ally's cause is understandable, since sophists could express well their constituents' views. Yet, even in such instances, rhetoric's power could be distorted and manipulated. As John Oscar Lofberg (1976: 68) noted while discussing sycophancy in Athens, "one of the methods employed by Athens in the government of the subject states was to require the allies to come to Athens for legal settlement of disputes." This process, well attested in Xenophon's *Polity of the Athenians* (1. 16), gave pro-Athenian sycophants the opportunity to parade their own interests under the name of democracy in legal and deliberative assemblies. In such instances presbyters were threatened with accusations of being enemies of democracy if they did not meet the demands of blackmailers. In the spirit of the McCarthy communist witch-hunts of the 1950s, sycophants exploited these alliances by threatening to prosecute subject allies and wealthy enemies as anti-democrats. In what would have been Plato's worst nightmare, many used the power of rhetoric in the deliberation of such alliances to extort, lobby and bribe (Xenophon, *Polity of the Athenians* 1. 16; Lofberg 1976: 69).

Magna Graecia and the Transformation of Hellenic Rhetoric to Rome

The Greek colonies in Sicily and Magna Graecia ("Great Greece" or southern Italy) evolved into established cities, many of which continued long after the Hellenic Period. Once viewed as subject allies to founding Greek city-states, these western cities became powerful in their own right, evolving into independence and self-government (Bourne 1966: 23). Their prosperity enabled them not only to persist but to sustain their viability as intellectual centers. The sophistic schools of rhetoric that began in these western Greek cities likewise grew in number and reputation. In addition to the Greek settlements, Italy was the site for a number of other peoples. The Etruscan people had developed an advanced civilization, and the ever-growing tribes of Italic people, such as the Latin tribes of Rome, were also emerging as forces in the West. From 509 B.C., the traditional date given to the founding of the Roman Republic, to 266 B.C., Rome began her active efforts to absorb, acquire and in some instances conquer the powerful Greek cities in Italy and Sicily. "It was with the western Greeks," wrote Boardman (1964: 175), "that the growing power of Rome first had to deal, and so to them in large part are due the continuity and transmission of Greek culture through Rome to the later western world." In 348 B.C. Rome secured an agreement with Carthage (Woodhead 1962: 175) that provided the opportunity to gain control of southern Italy and the West. Rome's preoccupation for control of Sicily and southern Italy accelerated as early as the fourth century B.C. and became active missions in the third century B.C. The Roman defeat of Greek Tarentum in 272 B.C. secured domination of Magna Graecia, and the defeat of the Carthagians in the First Punic War (264–241 B.C.) enabled Rome to acquire Sicily as her first colony (Polybius 1. 62–63).

The Roman victory at Tarentum had more significance than military conquest. It is clear that the conquering Romans were exposed to the Greek culture during their efforts in Magna Graecia. Livius Andronicus, the first Greek known to write in Latin, came to Rome in 272 B.C. from Tarentum (Gwynn 34). One of the soldiers serving under the Roman commander Fabius Maximus at Tarentum was Cato the Elder. Plutarch records in his account of the life of Cato that it was during this period that Cato became exposed to Greek education (*Cato Maior*). Cato became acquainted with the philosophy of the Pythagoreans of southern Italy as well as Greek literature. As we shall discuss later, Cato had strong views about "proper" Roman education and often was critical of Greek education. Yet, his knowledge of Greek rhetoric and literature is well attested. He was such a student of Demosthenes' oratory that he became known as the Roman Demosthenes (*Cato Maior*). In 204 B.C. Cato brought Ennius, the gifted Italian poet from Magna Graecia, back with him to Rome from Sardinia, where Ennius was serving in the army. Thoroughly educated in Greek, Ennius lectured in both Greek and Latin at Rome (Suetonius, *De Grammaticis* 1; Gwynn 35). By the closing of the second century B.C., the systems of Greek rhetoric were making an impact on Roman society. The impact of this phenomenon, as we shall also see, was well recognized by Romans other than just Cato. Even at this early stage—and even by the most stringent of Roman critics— the *"dunamis"* of Greek rhetoric was being felt in Rome.

Similar to the exposure to Greek culture that the Romans had at Tarentum, the "conquest" of Magna Graecia meant further assimilation of Greek systems of education. The nature and significance of this exposure is best realized through Rome's relationship with her Italian allies. Rome's alliances with Italian cities (*foedus*) meant not federation but absorption where the "allies" became a part of Rome. Those who did so voluntarily were viewed as equals (*foedus aequum*). This relationship between Rome and her Italian allies was tested in 90 B.C. when many Italian communities revolted after the assassination of their champion, Livius Drusus. Virtually all the Greek cities of southern Italy remained allies to Rome during the Italic or "Social War" of 90 B.C. and were rewarded for their loyalty. Romans passed the Julian Law, bestowing full citizenship to all communities that did not revolt (Appian, *Civil Wars* 1. 6. 49). Rome's successful suppression of this revolt did more than solidify her control over Italy; the consequence of uniform citizenship for all Italy south of the Po authorized the welding of a uniform culture.

Roman interaction with the landed tribes and Greek cities of Italy and Sicily greatly Hellenized Roman culture. Not only were Romans influenced by the century-long domination of the Hellenized Etruscans, but Roman interaction with Greek sites in southern Italy and Sicily over the centuries influenced her law, art, politics, religion and (eventually) the Roman acceptance of rhetoric. "First through the Etruscans and later by direct contact," Bourne (1966: 23) argues, "the Greeks of Italy and Sicily became the teachers of the Romans." Roman domination meant exposure. As Cicero so astutely observed in his *De Oratore* (2. 37), while Rome controlled the Greek West she also benefited from the interaction of Greek thought. In fact, Cicero's *In Verrem* provides an account of both his defense of the Sicilians against the ravages of their governor Gaius Verres and an indirect index of the value Rome felt for such acquisitions (Enos 1988; *In Verrem* 2. 1. 2–3.8, 13.2).

Polybius, the Greek historian from democratic Arcadia, witnessed first-hand the disintegration of Hellenistic kingdoms and Greek city-states during the first half of the second century B.C. The Roman sacking of Corinth in 146 B.C. was the *de facto* termination of the Archaean League marking the submission of the Greek world to Roman rule. As the foremost contemporary scholar and historian of the period, Polybius' comments on the consequences of the Roman conquest of Greece were particularly important for the history of rhetoric. Polybius noted that it was after the conquest of Greece that a significant number of sophists, especially those in rhetoric, flooded into Italy from Greece (39. 24). Polybius does not itemize the specific cities to which these Greek instructors immigrated, but there are two obvious choices. First, Rome was emerging as the political force and her ever increasing wealth and esteem for higher education made for an attractive center. "For it truly was no sort of shallow brook that flowed from Greece into our city," wrote Cicero, "but a mighty river of their education and art" (*De Republica* 2. 19. 34) Second, it is very likely that transplanted Greeks would seek out the Greek colonies in southern Italy of their mother cities and thus provide a renewed source for the already established schools of rhetoric. The implications of how prominent Greek thinkers influenced Roman attitudes toward literature and rhetoric will be discussed later. In fact, Polybius himself, admired by prominent Roman philhellenes such as Scipio, is the best illustration of the absorption and assimilation of Greek literary culture into Roman society.

The established schools of rhetoric populating Sicily and southern Italy were a clear influence on the education of Romans, the source for many of the pedagogues (e.g. Livy 5. 27–28), and a main source of their exposure to Hellenic rhetoric. Rhetoric worked its way up from the south into Rome, and there is little doubt of its presence at Rome by the early second century B.C. (Ennius, *Varia*, fr. 38, 5; Bonner 1977: 65). Western Greek schools of rhetoric eventually became so popular at Rome and—as we shall later discuss—so threatening to the patrician class that they were outlawed by the Senate (Suetonius, *De Rhetoribus*).

The evolution of rhetoric at Rome through western Greece compels us to reevaluate our present accounting of the transition from Greek to Roman rhetoric. Our popular accounts of the transition of Hellenic rhetoric to Roman rhetoric are often viewed as a transportation from Athens to Rome. That relationship must, at best, be seen as indirect and incomplete, if not imprecise. It is clear that rhetoric was introduced to Rome not merely by the few fortunate Romans—such as Cicero—who were able to travel to Athens, Rhodes and Asia Minor. Rather, the evidence shows a dramatically different phenomenon: rhetoric was introduced to Rome through western Greece. The schools of Sicily and Magna Graecia provided the exposure and interaction with Roman culture that introduced Greek rhetoric at Rome more so than by her few fortunate traveling citizens. The schools of sophistic declamation and rhetoric in the south moved north to Rome. By 161 B.C., Greek rhetoric became so influential that an edict banning its formal practice in Rome was passed (Suetonius, *De Rhetoribus*; Enos

1972). So pervasive was the Greek influence on Roman culture that reactionary Roman magistrates adopted the practice of never responding to Greeks except in Latin and even compelled Greeks to speak through an interpreter (Valerius Maximus, *Memorable Deeds and Sayings* 2. 2. 2).

Obviously, our history shows that such censoring of rhetoric, personal and institutionalized, failed at Rome. More importantly, it also reveals the source and nature of the influence of Greek rhetoric in Rome. The initial motivation and support for the expansion of democracy to aid Athenian imperialism used rhetoric as a tool. The sophists began a process that far eclipsed its original political intent. Rhetoric was firmly established in the West; its influence infiltrated a new political context and became a new source of political power in an emerging Roman Republic.

chapter 11

Kairos in the Roman Reception of Greek Rhetoric

> . . . the situation controls the rhetorical response in the same sense that the question controls the answer and the problem controls the solution. Not the rhetor and not persuasive intent, but the situation is the source and ground of rhetorical activity . . . (Lloyd Bitzer 1968:6).

The opportunity to study and develop skills in rhetoric systematically was a great benefit to ambitious Republicans. The study of Greek rhetoric exposed students to Greek thought and work. In addition, the systems of Greek rhetoric became the basis for Romans to develop their own Latin schools. These opportunities came not only from the individual Greek tutors and sophists who were attracted to Rome but also from the schools of declamation in southern Italy that spread their influence north. While educators and schools provided the opportunity to study rhetoric, that opportunity would not have been seized had not pragmatic Romans recognized its benefits. What social conditions in Republican Rome made the study of rhetoric so valuable? In short, it is important for us to understand the situation, or *kairos*, within which Roman rhetoric evolved from its Greek predecessor.

Recent interest in the concept of *kairos* has resulted in significant contributions of scholarly work (e. g. Kinneavy) about the importance of *kairos* as "context" in Hellenic rhetorical theory. The route to understanding rhetoric, whether in theory or practice, is through the environment within which it operates. Thus, when discussing situational factors involving rhetoric in Greece, historians will use the term *"kairos"* as a convenient and consistent label. Yet, each period and culture has its own situational forces that induce, constrain and influence discourse. The second major period in rhetoric's history, the Roman Republic, is no exception; here too situational forces must be considered in the shaping and influence of rhetoric. Unlike, her Greek predecessor, Roman rhetoric does not offer a complementary Latin term to the Greek *kairos.*

The life of the historian of rhetoric would be easier if Romans had either adopted the Greek term *kairos* wholesale or Latinized a parallel, equivalent term which could be conveniently substituted for its Hellenic counterpart. Then, when discussed by Romans, we would have a clear marker to indicate what Romans themselves thought was important to understand about the context within which their rhetoric was developed. Unfortunately, there are several candidates for the Roman equivalent of *kairos* but no one single term to be substituted. The temptation to substitute a Latin term as synonymous with *kairos* invites dangers of transfer. To first identify a term and then use that word as a lens to view the environment risks distortion through presupposition. The meaning of any abstract term is the echo of the meaning shaped through use. A more productive task, particularly at this stage, is to understand the Roman equivalent of *kairos* through an opposite route. That is, we need first to understand the conditions within which the study and practice of rhetoric emerged as well as the particular reception Romans gave to Greek rhetoric. Through an understanding of these conditions we will be better equipped to advance explanations for its impact. Building meaning through a reconstruction of the social, political and culture forces of the Roman Republic will provide a framework which will eventually help build our meaning of a Roman notion of *kairos.* We are also fortunate to have sufficient sources as evidence to weigh and sift, particularly the first-hand observations of Marcus Tullius Cicero (106–43 B.C.) and a number of Romans in the generations immediately following this important period. These sources permit us to synthesize and thereby advance an explanation of rhetoric situated in the Republic.

The Republic was a period in which rhetoric was important both in theory and practice. The formal study of Roman rhetoric was instituted during the Republic and, along with it, a concurrent exposure to Greek thought. The resulting schools of rhetoric played an increasingly important role in the education of Romans, and the practice of rhetoric was a powerful tool for social impact and political change. Arguments, both in matters of public policy and legal disputes, were presented in the Forum. The Curia was the site where senators—ranging in number from 100–900—gathered to deliberate on matters of public policy. The Forum was also the site for litigation. The courts commonly held multiple, simultaneous trials before active, vocal audiences. The courts and Senate were literally arenas for eloquence where decisions could be influenced by the power of argument.

Romans institutionalized the Senate and courts as formalized, communal mechanisms of *kairos*—that is, as sanctioned systems for providing a public environment within which problems could be resolved through discussion and debate. In this sense, Romans institutionalized *kairos* and sought to have a stable society within which such systems could operate by providing a formalized, *de facto kairos* for rhetorical discourse. Schools of rhetoric trained rhetors for effective discourse within such systems. Despite efforts to regularize the environment for rhetoric, social forces kept the Senate and the courts unstable. Realizing the fragility of this condition itself is part of understanding this particular *kairos*. When social forces act upon established civic forces in such a manner that the legitimate, legalized methods are compromised, the society itself risks not only the loss of rhetoric but of justice. Understanding the delicate balance between institutionalized *kairos* and external, social *kairos* is, then, the route to understanding the nature and impact of rhetoric during this period.

Cicero's career in politics, his skill as an orator, and his theoretical sensitivity as a rhetorician give us an invaluable perspective from which to observe this most rhetorical of social situations. While Cicero's views are not to be taken as the final voice simply because he expressed them, they nonetheless serve as a point of orientation, one which is grounded in real examples and first-hand accounts. It is not often in our studies in the history of rhetoric that we can have a source who is not only an active participant but also a keen observer of his own age—one who expresses those observations in terms that help reconstruct the role that rhetoric played in the process. Although Cicero is not the only voice on matters of rhetoric for his age, as will be apparent, he does occupy a central position in the analysis of how rhetoric operated in his society.

Rhetoric's Emergence as a Discipline in the Roman Republic

Despite the attractive qualities of rhetoric, its reception was not an uninterrupted, smooth progression. Just as the social forces

From the A. F. Sochatoff Collection.

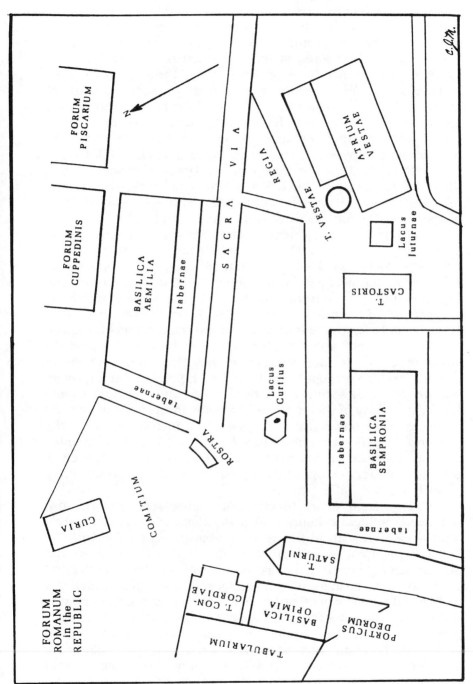

Permission granted by the American Classical League.

buffeting Rome were unstable, so were attitudes toward rhetoric. Roman patricians had all the fears and apprehensions toward the formal study of rhetoric and its merits as a serious discipline in the education of their children as did their Athenian counterparts three hundred years earlier. Romans compounded these reservations by a strong anti-Hellenic sentiment which they associated with the study of rhetoric. Roman Republicans of the second century B.C. characterized themselves as having a rigid intolerance for anything but the most pristine Roman values of clear, direct discourse and a simplified purity of the Latin tongue (Quintilian 9. 4. 3, 4; Cicero, *De Oratore* 1. 14). The reception of Greek rhetoric (Cicero, *Tusculanae Disputationes* 1. 5) as a formal discipline was strongly opposed because it was thought to be both self-indulgent and supportive of Greek customs over Roman practices.

As we shall see in subsequent chapters, early Romans saw the increasing popularity of Greek-based rhetoric as a threat to the pristine values embedded in Roman education and, as a result, enacted two forms of legislation intended to outlaw its study. The first, a *Senatus Consultum* issued in 161 B.C. expressly prohibited the teaching of rhetoric in Rome by Greek sophists (Suetonius, *De Rhetoribus* 1). Restrictions on Greek-based rhetoric had little effect, particularly since Latin schools emerged that merely adapted the Greek principles to the Latin vernacular. These Latin schools of rhetoric became so popular in their own right that Romans were required to issue a second restriction. The second effort to eliminate the formal study of rhetoric in Rome came in the form of an edict in 92 B.C. (Suetonius, *De Rhetoribus* 1); in this instance, the censors Gnaeus Domitius Ahenobarbus and Lucius Licinius Crassus published a statement of condemnation for the Latin schools of rhetoric, citing their concerns over the moral propriety of such a system of education.

This second effort to eliminate schools of rhetoric also overcame political censure and restrictions so that by Cicero's youth—as he reveals in the opening passages of his *De Amicitia* (1. 1)—rhetorical education not only existed but appeared standardized. In not much more than one generation after the first prohibition, the hostile environment for schools of rhetoric changed and with it the view of its utility. For a young Cicero, rhetoric was the key ingredient for the operation of a successful Rome, the basis from which civic operations could serve as a normative and regulatory function. Cicero's youthful treatises, particularly *De Inventione* (1. 1–2) capture well not only the importance of rhetorical education but the place of rhetoric itself in Roman society. For a youthful, innocent Cicero the ability of expression was the tie binding the society, the vehicle for transmitting wisdom and the force holding the city together.

Donald C. Bryant once defined rhetoric as the art of "adjusting ideas to people and of people to ideas" (1965:19). We have seen much the same sort of malleability in Greek rhetoric. As seen earlier, the "art" of Greek rhetoric was introduced to Rome primarily through Greek schools of rhetoric and declamation that came from the western Greek cities of Sicily and southern Italy. The "art" of this Greek rhetoric, however, was developed in response to Greek social and political needs. These *technai* or systems were sustained because of their utility. One of rhetoric's persistent characteristics, and the principle reason for its endurance, is its plasticity. That is, principles of rhetoric are grounded in their sensibility and use in the societies within which they function. Rhetoric is always under a state of metamorphoses, adapting tenets and heuristics to meet immediate problems that can be resolved by discourse. When introduced into Roman society, "Greek" rhetoric began such a transformation. Those features of Greek rhetoric that were particularly suited to Roman society gained popularity and widespread usage while other features of Greek rhetoric, less relevant to immediate, pragmatic needs, were correspondingly de-emphasized. Thus, Roman rhetoric is the evolutionary consequence of those features of Greek rhetoric that best "fit" solutions to Rome's systems and problems. Certainly not all needs generated by Romans could be satisfied by re-tooling Greek rhetoric. Roman rhetoricians such as Cicero and Quintilian created their own theories to address Roman exigencies. Yet, as we shall see in chapter 4, Cicero, Quintilian and virtually every other prominent Roman rhetorician makes evident—either explicitly or indirectly—an indebtedness to Greek rhetoric. What makes Roman rhetoric "Roman" is not its autonomy from Greek rhetoric but rather its adaptation to current needs. Thus, to understand the debates about "Roman" rhetoric in such works as Cicero's *De Oratore*, it is important to understand both how rhetoric was a source of power in Roman society and the *kairos* within which it operated. By understanding the Roman *dunamis* of rhetoric, we will be better able to understand those aspects of Roman rhetoric that became dominant in their culture.

The Realities of Roman Society for Rhetoric

The Roman Republic was a period of both stabilization of institutions and social revolution. The transition of Rome from a primitive kingship to a Republic and the attendant military success associated with the consecutive victories in the Punic Wars stabilized the Senatorial power of the patrician (aristocratic) class and created an attendant economic prosperity that increased the power and influence of the commercially-oriented equestrian (upper-middle class) order. The enfranchisement of Italy, the conquests of war and commerce added to the wealth and numbers of the equestrian class, so that by the first century B.C. they had evolved from their founding number of 300 to over 1800 officially enrolled members of the *ordo. Equites* became close in social status to the patrician senators, and their joint sharing of property and commerce created a plutocracy. The plebian class also benefited, albeit indirectly, from Rome's success. Military victories and economic prosperity justified an expanding military—which required, in turn, mass participation and resulted in larger solicitation of plebians, thus nurturing yet another source of power.

Control over the power to set policy and adjudicate legal decisions served more than a need to regulate Rome's everyday affairs; it became the source for legitimate political control. Restricted access to such power was illustrated in a number of ways. Annual elections of the two consuls—the highest political office during the Republic—was limited to a tight circle of a few patrician families. In fact, Cicero's consulship in 63 B.C. was the first instance in which a "new man" was elected consul in three decades (Syme 1963: 94). Control of the courts was an on-going battle in the Republic, with the patrician class and the equestrian order yielding control to the other only out of duress or as a penalty for corruption and bribery. Even the establishment and interpretation of laws has a history of struggle between the classes. The patrician class for years refused to even publish the Twelve Tables governing Roman law but rather kept them within their collective "oral" memory and thereby retained the power of interpretation and control. The inscribing of these laws (451 B.C.) and the increasing sophistication of legislation is testimony to the yielding and censure of power through legalized offices.

The courts during the Roman Republic were strongly influenced by political and social forces. Almost fifty years before Cicero's birth, the tribune Lucius Calpurnius Piso Frugi secured the enactment of his *Lex Pecuniis Repetundis* (149 B.C.) which firmly established a court for extortion cases (*questio*). The standing commission for this court was entrusted to the Senate, which was greatly influenced by *nobiles* or patricians. Two decades later, however, the popular leader Gaius Gracchus sponsored his *Lex Iudiciaria*, which shifted the control of the courts away from the

Senate to the wealthiest non-patrician class, the *equites*. This transfer of power between social classes not only shifted control of the courts but intensified already strained relations between the patrician-dominated Senate and the *equites*, a condition which lasted well into the late Republic (Scullard). Such tumultuous events meant that the courts were a constantly changing audience and that each trial was presented in ever-changing social constraints. Several of Cicero's arguments reveal a sensitivity to the composition of listeners and to the political forces which stood ready to interpret the larger social implications of the trial.

It would be difficult to overstate these political constraints on legal rhetoric; the courts had been manipulated by party politics for generations. Quintus Servilius Caepio, consul in 196 B.C., passed a compromise law which provided for juries composed of senators and *equites*. About 101 B.C., the orator Gaius Servius Glaucia helped enact a law restoring the courts for extortion (*repetundae*) and their management, or quaestorship, to the *equites*. Further reforms were attempted in 91 B.C. when the tribune Livius Drusus tried to elevate three hundred *equites* to the Senate and in c. 89 B.C. by the tribune Marcus Silvanus Platius, who introduced a *Lex Iudiciaria* which promoted mixed rather than equestrian juries. Certainly efforts at reform were made, but such changes only dramatized the political and social implications of legal argument. One of the most significant reforms of the courts came during the early years of Cicero's career, when Sulla's conservative revolution and legislative programs of 81 B.C. returned the power of the six hundred members by promoting *equites* who supported him. Sulla delegated all the trial cases (*quaestiones*) to the senators. The institution of Sullan reform gave the Senate the exclusive right to supply juries and control over at least seven permanent *quaestiones* which covered all major crimes: murder and poisoning, forgery, extortion, treason, electoral bribery, peculation, and assault (Scullard 1963: 86).

Later reforms modified Sulla's conservative reform of the courts. Lucius Aurelius, praetor in 70 B.C., tempered Sulla's legal reforms by passing the *Lex Aurelia Iudiciaria*, which allowed the juries of criminal courts to consist of an equal number of senators, *equites*, and *tribuni aerarii*, by creating three panels or *decuriae* of three hundred members each. The *tribuni aerarii* were citizens whose property qualifications were immediately below the Equestrian Order, and their affiliation was with the *equites* rather than the Senatorial Order. The *tribuni aerarii* were temporarily suppressed by Caesar, but while an active force, their support of the *equites* provided a two-thirds domination of the courts over the patricians of the Senate, which violated the spirit (if not the letter) of the Sullan reforms. During Cicero's legal career, factions of the Senate and *equites* continued to struggle for domination of the courts, which each group recognized as a source of political power. The influence of this struggle is apparent throughout Cicero's advocacy, for his career spanned the period from Sulla to Caesar and paralleled an era of transition in the power of legal oratory in the State and in the party politics of the courts. The necessity of careful preparation for a career in this turbulent profession underscores the critical importance and popularity of rhetorical training in Rome.

Increased affluence and the attendant party politics provided situational factors that supported the study of rhetoric. A large number of wealthy families could offer their children the benefits of educational opportunities. Educators, often Greek slaves, provided instruction both at home and in schools. The courts and politics both were institutions that provided a natural arena for the practice of rhetoric. Trial-by-jury and policy-by-vote provided the natural conditions for justifying the study of rhetoric as a way of enhancing expression for the purposes of securing assent. Rhetoric facilitated public advancement, and the ties between Roman courts and politics were closer than the professed separation of the two in contemporary society. It was possible for Romans who were facile with expression to use their ability in rhetoric to personal advantage. In the courts, advocates who successfully represented influential *clientelae* would be able to see these same individuals as personal *patroni* who could facilitate political advancement through the *cursus honorum*, the standard progression of public offices leading to and culminating in the consulship. Cicero's career was the most successful illustration of this phenomenon, but other young advocates enjoyed sufficient success to make clear the political advantages of mastering rhetoric. As an office-holder, in turn, the political assembly would provide an arena other than the courts for the force of effective eloquence of causes. In essence then, a climate, or *kairos*, existed in Rome that was conducive to the application of rhetorical skills as a source of power. While the realization of this power was made possible because of the existence of institutions and procedures that invited rhetoric, other forces were concurrently in operation which would alter that situation and, in turn, the environment for rhetoric.

Rhetoric as an Emerging Source of Power in the Roman Republic

As we learned earlier, there were three traditional qualifications which aided a young Roman in acquiring political power in the Republic: wealth, an aristocratic heritage, and military sagacity. Lacking these conventional routes to power, ambitious Republicans could utilize one further avenue of success: the power of rhetoric. The schools of Greek and later Roman declamation that flourished at Rome trained young Romans in effective political and legal deliberation. Since political policy and legal verdicts were grounded in the assent of the audience, those individuals who could be effective in suasory discourse enjoyed a decided advantage in such arenas. As mentioned earlier, Cicero established a reputation and earned the political support to be elected consul through his skill as a forensic orator (Syme 1963: 94). The relationship between rhetoric and its pragmatic application as a source of power in Roman society was a necessary outgrowth of the endemic relationship between politics and law at Rome.

Talent in oral argument could be used efficiently in the courts. Although proficiency in oral discourse earned immediate victories and a word-of-mouth reputation, no artifacts of talent would endure to sustain a reputation. Composing forensic rhetoric after the trial, however, provided enduring evidence that continually enhanced an orator's reputation. After the current interest surrounding a trial and its issues waned, published orations remained visible and included legal accounts of a trial as well as commentaries on social and political conditions. In time, the "text" of forensic compositions such as Cicero's changed as the context changed so that the essays came to be viewed less as legal documents and more as vehicles for social commentary and political advancement. Proficiency in oral argument helped orators acquire reputations, but composing skills helped to sustain reputations (Enos 1988).

Young Romans used such reputations to establish *clientelae* who would advance political careers. Cicero's career is an excellent illustration of this condition. A brief account of Cicero's advocacy underscores the importance of his oral and written legal skills in the politics of Roman society. In 75 B.C., at the earliest legal age, Cicero was elected *quaestor* for a one-year term in western Sicily. One of the primary benefits which he felt this office gave him was the right to express his opinions in the Senate (*In Verrem* 2. 5. 36). Through such early defense cases as his *Pro Quinctio* and *Pro Roscio Amerino*, his successful prosecution of the proconsul Gaius

Verres in 70 B.C., and his deliberative orations against Catiline as consul in 63 B.C., Cicero established himself as a leading advocate and politician in Rome.

The contribution of oratory to Cicero's legal and political career was best summarized by his brother Quintus, who emphasized that "whoever you are, you are from this" (Quintus Cicero, *Commentariolum Petitionis* 2). Besides believing that oratory had always exercised great influence, Cicero professed an elitist position on the qualifications of a rhetor (*Brutus* 39). "Out of all those individuals who have undertaken very liberal studies and instruction," he wrote, "a small number of outstanding poets and orators have stood out" (*De Oratore* 1. 7). Cicero believed that "everyone had an interest in speaking," but that the qualifications for successful oratory were so stringent that it was easier to become a general than an accomplished pleader (*Brutus* 182; *De Oratore* 1. 7).Cicero felt that he had to compensate for his lack of nobility and developed his ability as an advocate so that he could establish *clientelae* who would advance him politically.

Politics had a definite impact on the court, an impact which often resulted in judicial corruption. The oligarchical control of the courts by the patricians excluded the voice of the populace, and since the leading political offices were dominated by these *nobiles*, unchecked politics in the courts resulted in corruption. A clear example of such corruption came in Cicero's youthful defense of Sextus Roscius in 80 B.C. Cicero remarked that he was virtually the only orator courageous enough to risk Sulla's displeasure and to undertake the defense (Cicero, *Pro Roscio Amerino* 5; Aulus Gellius, *Noctes Atticae* 15. 28). The primary reason for the unpopularity of the case was that the prosecution consisted of colleagues of Sulla, who was then in his second consulship. The fear of the jurors that a verdict against one of Sulla's men could be taken personally by the consul was so strong that Cicero had to devote part of his case to reminding them of their obligations to justice (*Pro Roscio Amerino* 8). In spite of the intimidation by the prosecution, Cicero was able to win the case by carefully incriminating Sulla's men while praising Sulla himself (*Pro Roscio Amerino* 6, 127, 131).

By the time of Cicero's prosecution of the proconsul Gaius Verres in 70 B.C., the corruption of the Senatorial courts had greatly increased. Despite Verres' considerable influence within the patrician class and the oratorical brilliance of his advocate Hortensius, Cicero was able to secure a charge of extortion from the aristocratic jury. Cicero indicated throughout the prosecution that this case was not only a trial of Verres but of the fitness of the Senatorial Order to engage in court management. Sulla's conservative reforms had removed the fifty-year control of the law courts from the Equestrian Order, but the Senate was hard-pressed to match the reputation for fairness that the Equestrian Order had earned. Cicero urged the senators to invoke their power and "blot out and remove the disgrace and infamy taken on by this Order through the years" or else risk having men continue to think "that a completely different Order [Equestrian] for judging matters ought to be sought" (*In Verrem* 1. 49). Cicero's purpose was to have his senatorial jurors believe that the entire revamping of the courts hinged on the outcome of this trial, and he even emphasized that Pompey and the *Populares* already had enough force to change the jury composition to represent levels of Roman citizenship (*In Verrem* 1. 45). In essence, Cicero realized the need for an honest jury, since it would determine "whether in the case of this man it can be established that a very criminal and very wealthy individual can be condemned by a senatorial court" (*In Verrem* 1. 47). Cicero's strategy was to convince the judges of the discredit which all senators would share by acquitting a known criminal.

Cicero continued to enhance his forensic and political reputation after the Verrine orations and moved through his *cursus honorum* to the consulship in 63 B.C. During this seven-year period, the rising power of the *Populares* held increasing importance to Caesar, Pompey and Crassus. The courts were not freed from the factions which continued to fight for supremacy. The Ciceronian ideal of a stable court functioning in a tranquil state faced a major challenge: the conspiracy of Catiline. Several senators from well-established patrician families saw the emerging power of non-aristocrats as a threat. Lead by Catiline and his associates, a reactionary conspiracy was plotted which was intended to re-establish conservative control of Rome. Catiline, who was tolerated if not supported by Caesar and Crassus, was defeated by Cicero in the consular elections and organized a conspiracy which Cicero suppressed. There is little doubt that if Catiline had been successful, one of his first acts as a patrician and former Sullan supporter would have been to transfer the power of the courts back to the Senatorial Order. Cicero himself admitted in 63 B.C. that the courts were disorganized and vulnerable to the kind of strong-arm reform that had occurred two decades earlier (*De Lege Agraria* 2. 8). Further-more, Cicero maintained in his *Paradoxa Stoicorum* that the law courts were all but nonexistent when the State was torn apart by the conspiracy because the laws lacked force and the courts were corrupted (27). Consequently, Cicero believed that his efforts against Catiline had preserved the stability of the State and allowed the courts to function in a climate of justice and equity (*Epistulae ad Atticum* 1. 16). Such action earned Cicero the esteem and *vir bonus* image imperative for political advancement.

The suppression of the Catilinarian conspiracy, however, did not thwart other forces attempting to seize control and to misuse the courts as a means of gaining political power. For Cicero, the abuse of forensic oratory was personified in Publius Clodius Pulcher. In May 61 B.C., Cicero presented convincing evidence that Clodius had violated the sanctity of the *Bona Dea* festival. When Clodius was narrowly acquitted by the jury which Crassus had bribed, Cicero wrote to Atticus, "immediately after the acquittal of Clodius, I observed the frivolity and weakness of the courts" (*Epistulae ad Atticum* 1. 19). He became increasingly disenchanted with the political climate and concentrated on litigation. In 59 B.C. Cicero again wrote to Atticus saying "I . . . attend no public affairs and direct all my work and effort to my forensic duty" (*Epistulae ad Atticum* 2. 23). When Cicero's advocacy was interrupted by his exile in 58 B.C.—an exile which was secured through Clodius' tribuneship—the juries ceased to function and (consequently) pronounced no verdicts (*Post Reditum in Senatu 6*). Corruption was, at best, only suspended. Cicero's letters of 54 B.C. provide testimony to the renewed activity of the courts where more than one trial of *praevaricatio*, or fraudulent mismanagement of a case, occurred (*Epistulae ad Familares* 8. 8.2; *Epistulae ad Quintum Fratem* 2. 16. 3).

After his return from exile, Cicero continued his forensic activity, observing that the Forum was unusually peaceful (*Epistulae ad Quintum Fratem* 2. 16. 1; 3. 6. 4; 2. 15a. 5). He believed, however, that this tranquility was actually "more civil senility than acquiescence," and that its probable cause was the emergence of a dictatorship (*Epistulae ad Quintum Fratem* 2. 15a. 5). By October 54 B.C., Cicero had resigned himself to believing that an effective Republic, Senate and law courts had ceased to exist, although he was active in the courts that year, winning his case for Vatinius and losing his defense of Gabinius. Cicero's last major forensic effort prior to the Civil War of 52 B.C. was his unsuccessful defense of Milo, who was impeached for the murder of Clodius. During the prelude to the Civil War, the traditional sources of power were being consolidated under a few individuals and eventually became embodied under one dynast: Gaius Julius Caesar.

Cicero had mixed opinions concerning the courts under Caesar. In letters to his friends, he made no secret of his sorrow over the loss of the Republic and admitted to one colleague that "nothing is more dear to me than the Republic herself" (*Epistulae ad Familiares* 2. 15. 3; 6. 21. 3; 7. 28. 3). In his *De Republica*, Cicero argued that man was in concord through speech and that it was the right of the people to be masters of the laws and courts (3. 3; 1. 48). To Cicero, Caesar's control of the courts fell far short of this ideal. There was some indication that Cicero initially believed Caesar might use his power to stabilize the courts after the bloodshed of the Civil War, and the court cases judged by Caesar (*Pro Ligario* and *Pro Rege Deiotaro*) reinforce the impression of his idealism (*Pro Marcello* 23). Cicero soon realized, however, that Caesar used the courts to further his own political ends. A letter to Atticus explaining his responses to a plea from a relative of Caesar to defend him indicated Cicero's embitterment: "I replied to him that he had no need for a counsel, since Caesar, a relative of his, was all-powerful; nevertheless, I am going to support him" (*Epistulae ad Atticum* 12. 49).

After the death of Caesar, men such as Mark Antony so thoroughly attempted to corrupt the courts that Cicero recommended they be closed (*Orationes Philippicae* 6. 2). Disillusioned, embittered, and believing that the courts were abolished in all but name, Cicero sought retirement from public affairs: "For seeing that it wearied me earlier, when age and ambition motivated me, and I was in short, permitted not to defend whom I did not wish to defend but at this time life is of no account. Actually, I do not anticipate any reward for my effort, and I feel that I am compelled to defend a number of men, whose merits do not deserve my best efforts, at the request of those who have merited well. And so in my judgment, I seek at last every reason for living as I see fit" (*Epistulae ad Familiares* 7. 1. 4-5). Cicero's death by proscription ended the life of one of Rome's most famous advocates—and represented the end of Republican rhetoric.

Rhetoric, Unity and Justice

Cicero's life is a testimonial to resourcefulness. Denied access to many of the traditional sources of power in Roman society, Cicero created his own. He utilized his compositional skills to produce legal orations which became the medium for his political advancement, catapulting him to the forefront of political life. There is no doubt that Cicero was sensitive to the power that forensic rhetoric had on Roman society. In an age when advocates were tempted to compromise ethical standards for political expediency and when charges of bribery and corruption (*maiestas*) were common, Cicero praised the legal profession as the foundation of divinely guided practical wisdom which ordered Rome (*Epistulae ad Familiares* 3. 11. 2; *Pro Balbo* 31). In his *De Officiis*, he portrayed forensic orators as guardians of the civil law whose obligation was to maintain the tranquility of the State (2. 65-68). This commitment to public service was ascribed by the ancients as the primary duty of civil professions (2. 66). "Favors and patronage are extensively accessible therefore to an eloquent man," wrote Cicero, "when he genuinely works and when, in accordance with ancient practices, he assumes the defense cases of many with seriousness and gratitude" (2. 66).

Cicero saw eloquence as the force which bound society and the establishment of law as the mechanism which sustained this unity and allowed Romans to recognize order in their existence (*De Inventione* 1. 2; *De Natura Deorum* 2. 154). The obligation of sustaining legal order in the society was delegated to the forensic orator. The role of forensic activity, however, was not to establish tranquility in society but rather to sustain it. "For indeed," Cicero maintained, "the desire for speaking is not customarily waged" nor "when hindered and bound by the tyranny of a king; eloquence is the follower of peace and the ally of leisure and, in an already well-ordered state, a sort of foster-child" (*Brutus* 45). Free speech could flourish only when questions of justice were resolved in the courts and not on the battlefield (*Orator* 141; *De Oratore* 1. 14).

For rhetoric to perform such functions, however, required an environment that could support both standards and consequences for failing to meet the standards. When Rome changed from Republic to Empire, rhetoric lost the environment that made it a source of political power. While proficiency in rhetoric continued to be an advantage in legal practice throughout the Empire, it is clear that rhetoric's educational mission shifted and the pragmatic orientation of Republican schools of declamation correspondingly shifted in emphasis to the appreciation of rhetoric for its aesthetic features. As we will see in subsequent chapters, attitudes toward rhetoric changed. By the Empire, schools of rhetoric that had once been called into existence for pragmatic training in language arts became associated with excessive display of eloquence, a consequence that was a reflection of the place that rhetoric was now seen to occupy in a society that had dramatically altered its politics.

The role of rhetoric within a Republic in revolution tells us much about the concepts of justice and equity. To Cicero, justice (*iustitia*) was most often manifested in the advocate by his attempts to attain equity (*aequitas*)—the aim of the courts (*Partitiones Oratoriae* 130; *De Oratore* 1. 141; *De Inventione* 2. 156). Both equity and justice are terms which Cicero used to indicate a condition of balance or tranquility. Rhetoric served both normative and regulatory functions within the Republic. Through the Senate, laws could be enacted that would seek to provide a standard of values. Through the courts, breaches of those standards would be adjudicated in systematic ways. The objective of litigation was the attainment of equity, to readjust an imbalance through an interpretation of existing laws on a particular issue. Justice, however, implied a far more generic balance than the equity of individual cases; it was the virtuous condition of balance upon which a society was built. Nevertheless, a "just" orator who continually strove for equity within the courts was also contributing to the maintenance of moral balance for the State. In this respect, Ciceronian equity was the foundation of statecraft. Justice was the highest virtue. Justice combined with equity were principal ingredients for making citizens "good men" (*viri boni*) and strong factors in promoting and strengthening society (*De Officiis* 2. 83; 1. 20; 1. 100; *De Finibus* 5. 65).

Not only did Cicero frequently mention in his private correspondence how critical it was that matters be settled through deliberation rather than conflict (*Epistulae ad Familares* 7. 2) but that the public not abuse that privilege (*Epistulae ad Familares* 11. 12). Cicero's remarks reveal an astute sensitivity to the delicate balance necessary to attain a *kairos* that would permit conflict to be resolved through rhetoric. There is no doubt that the Roman audience was notorious for their wild displays of emotion (Carcopino 187, 188 ff.) and unhesitatingly heckled even the most powerful of Romans (*Epistulae ad Familares* 1. 5b). Yet, it was precisely this climate that provided the semi-controlled chaos (*Epistulae ad Atticum* 14. 11) for unfettered deliberation. The active participation of the audience could well be a sign of their engagement—as well as their often unreserved, spontaneous judgment—that any rhetor must take as a factor. In short, the *kairos* within which rhetoric operated provided the atmosphere within which disputes could be publicly displayed and, in an agnostic struggle for survival, the rhetor with the strongest appeal to the listeners triumphed.

While this environment allowed—and even prompted—tumultuous moments, its ends were justice and peace. It is difficult to read a treatise by Cicero and not see the notion of justice as a central concept. In *Partitiones Oratoriae* (78) Cicero saw justice as the manifestation of a society's virtue. In *De Officiis* (1. 100) he considered justice as the way in which a society strengthens itself and, consequently, its foundation (2. 83). On a personal level, Cicero considered justice to be a state of mind (*De Inventione* 2. 160), a quality that separates humans from other creatures and unites

them with the gods (*De Natura Deorum* 2. 62; *De Republica* 6. 13).
Cicero believed that justice comes after a society's institutions are
stabilized (*Brutus* 45) and, within that environment, is preserved
by its laws and their enforcement (*De Legibus* 1.18-19).

Justice and equity were elements in Cicero's supreme law:
reason (*De Legibus* 1. 21, 23; *Partitiones Oratoriae* 78). In essence,
Cicero's law was the natural intelligence of humans which provided
the basis for a just society; ignorance, or one's failure in natural
intelligence, necessitated the reinstatement of equity through
litigation (*De Legibus* 1. 18, 19). One task of the advocate, then,
was to interpret the conditions of a case to his listeners. Because
auditors needed to understand as a prerequisite to determining
validity, the pleader occasionally sacrificed eloquence for the sake
of clarifying reason (*De Legibus* 1. 19).

Despite his idealization of justice, however, Cicero recognized
that justice could not be considered an end in itself (*De Legibus* 1.
53). The "favor" (*iucunditas*) which a just orator elicited was the
basic virtue which allowed him to be considered a "good man" (*vir
bonus*) in the eyes of the audience. Thus, the concept of being
morally just was not an ideal without a practical referent but rather
a means of gaining honorable distinction (*gloria*) through the *vir
bonus* character. In Cicero's concept of forensic rhetoric, then, law,
justice and equity served both as guardians of social values and
keepers of the peace and provided the practical regard of public
recognition, which often lead to more power within the Republic.

This examination of Cicero's views on the Republic and
rhetoric's operation within law and politics explains why Romans
found the principles of Greek rhetoric so attractive and why many
were eager to apply those principles to a rhetoric suited to their
needs. First, Cicero's extensive legal training reveals a thorough
preparation in oral and written composition and a sensitivity to the
respective advantages they could offer in the Roman Republic.
Second, various political factions recognized the advantage of
controlling the courts and fought for domination prior to and
throughout Cicero's career. In fact, Cicero's career as an advocate
paralleled an era of transition in the courts of Rome, spanning the
dynasts from Sulla to Caesar and a struggle between the Senatorial
and Equestrian Orders for judicial control. Third, Republican
Romans recognized in the principles of Greek rhetoric a source of
political power in their own society. Young Romans who secured
legal victories for influential clients achieved public offices. Cicero,
a *novus homo* lacking patrician birth, military talent, and wealth—
the conventional sources of power for political advancements—
concentrated his effort in forensic rhetoric and gained enough

success to secure the consulship in 63 B.C. Fourth and last, Cicero believed that oratory is the force that binds a society and aids in maintaining an already-existing tranquil state—but does not create a peaceful state out of discord. Cicero also maintained that justice and equity, aspects of the supreme law of reason, were parts of a conceptual method for resolving failures of natural intelligence. Ignorance necessitated litigation in order to resolve conflict by acquiring knowledge. Furthermore, Cicero maintained that justice was not an end in itself but a method for preserving a stable society and a means of gaining popular favor for the advocate, the image of the *vir bonus*. Writing and publishing his legal orations then served not only his political advancement but, ideally, sustained harmony by preserving opinions about social conduct.

Rhetoric and the Emergence of the Roman Dynasts

Ironically, the same prosperity and military success that stabilized the Roman Republic and increased the importance of rhetoric also contributed to the demise of both. A generation before Cicero, the liberal Gracchi and the arch-conservative Sulla Felix demonstrated how effective a force the military could be in influencing Roman society. Ongoing military enterprises (and the private wealth to support them) resulted in large, well-trained armies loyal to the individuals who controlled them. The wealth acquired from successful military campaigns rapidly evolved in Darwin-like fashion; those generals who were brilliant in military strategy increased in wealth and resources to the point where they could challenge even the most affluent Roman patricians. These dynasts not only grew in personal power but their political preferences attracted followers who supported their views. The ideological and physical clashes of the conservative *Optimates* and liberal *Populares* were the political realization of the concentration of power held by few individuals. The first (and unsanctioned) Triumvirate—Pompey, Caesar and Crassus (60 B.C.)—constituted the evolution of political forces brought into existence by the survival of the best of military genius, political sagacity and personal wealth. While overtures to preserving the legal and civic procedures of Rome were continually expressed, the concentration of power among so few resulted in the deterioration of communal power in all but appearance.

The struggle for political power among factions at Rome occupied the lives of the final two generations of Republicans, ending only with the emergence of Octavius (later Augustus, 23 B.C.—14 A.D.) as the *Princeps* or "first among equals." During these disruptive decades, parties mouthed allegiance to the Republican forms of government and courts and justified actions "in the name of" the Republic, but the consequence of these turbulent events was a shift of power which directly altered the civic, legal and political functions of Rome. These changes affected the environment for rhetoric and caused a shift in rhetoric itself. The most articulate eye-witness of these events was Cicero. Watching the rise of dynasts, the chaos of civil war and the erosion of Republican government and courts moved Cicero to advance observations on the nature and conditions of rhetoric. Cicero believed that rhetoric was a potent force in a stable Republic. The opportunity to secure assent through discourse provided the participatory activity that met the goals of Republican Rome. The shift of power into the hands of a few put such collective procedures at risk, directly altering the *kairos* in which rhetoric could function.

Cicero's views on justice within society tell us much about the notion of *kairos* within his Republic. Rhetoric was the instrument by which Romans were able to preserve and regulate a Republican form of government. The active participation of the community not only was important because the public adjudicated the validity of its rhetorical discourse but because they shared the goal of eloquence. In this sense, however, eloquence had a very specific meaning; that is, the articulation of wisdom with a passion for justice to audiences that could enact their own convictions. The more fractionalized the *kairos*, the greater the intensity for Republican eloquence. Cicero's orations against Catiline, for example, illustrate how eloquence itself could be a force in preserving the stability of the Republic and averting a civil war. There may be many other environments where eloquence had such a pragmatic and utilitarian function, but it was achieved in the Republic because the environment for it had been created and normalized. It was for this very reason that Plutarch praised Cicero, for he showed Romans how eloquence in a stable environment could make justice triumph.

Cicero believed that rhetoric could not operate under conditions where individual power suppressed Republican procedures. For Cicero, rhetoric served as a normative and regulatory force when a society was stable enough to permit its unfettered operation and willingly chose to adhere to its consequences. When systems allowing freedom of expression collapsed, he believed that rhetoric could do little or nothing to alter the situation. Cicero believed rhetoric operating in a system marked by tyranny was unlikely to alter the environment to induce a shift back to Republicanism. His letters to friends (*Epistulae ad Familares* 7. 28; 11. 14; 9. 18) reveal his bitterness over the constraints on the courts and Senate which he believed meant nothing less than the loss of the Republic.

Cicero's eloquent *Philippics* (*Orationes Philippicae*) proved the accuracy of his views. Cicero's passionate statements of outrage against the tyranny of Mark Antony are enshrined as masterpieces of rhetorical excellence and have long been used as models of eloquence. Yet, the ultimate effect of the *Philippics* was to so incense Antony that he placed Cicero's name on his proscription list for murder. When Antony placed Cicero's dismembered head and hands on the Rostra as a mocking symbol of his disdain for Cicero's "power" of rhetoric, he indirectly symbolized the fears Cicero had expressed. For all of Cicero's ability, the political conditions of Rome were such that even his eloquence could not overcome the forces which were in operation. Even the best rhetoric from Cicero proved to be ineffective, because the conditions for its impact were nonexistent. There need be no greater demonstration of the importance of *kairos* in Cicero's Republic than to compare the futility of his *Philippics* with his earlier triumph, *In Catilinam*. Cicero's speeches against Catiline were done under conditions where legal actions could be taken to avert civil war, and Cicero appealed to the Senate to take such action. The *Philippics*, however, were uttered when the consolidated power of a few men destroyed the normal environment for eloquence because there were (effectively) no organizational bodies to take action. Thus, justice was triumphant in the case of Catiline and humiliated in the case of the *Philippics* because there was no empowered audience to enact their conviction for Cicero's eloquence. It was the lack of *kairos* that ultimately prompted historians of rhetoric to see Cicero's masterful orations against Antony as eloquent failures, and the orations against Catiline as hallmarks in the history of justice. The *kairos* of each indirectly controlled the eloquence, if eloquence is judged in terms of its success in motivating society for the betterment of those involved in adjudicating its validity.

Conclusion: A Post-Ciceronian Epilogue on *Kairos*

Roman historians of rhetoric—past and present—mark the death of Cicero as both the end of the Republic and the end of rhetoric as a political force in Roman society. The stabilization of politics and society under the Augustan Principate correspondingly signals a shift of rhetoric from a source of power through free speech to an educational subject, facilitating learning and synonymous with the acquisition of literacy and subsequently culture. Augustus himself (Suetonius, *Divus Iulius*) believed that Cicero's ability in rhetoric was missed, and Tacitus' *Dialogus* is as much a statement of the loss of eloquence as it is a lament of the passing of Cicero. Quintilian's remarks on Cicero's suasory abilities unequivocally add to these testimonials, for much of the *Institutio Oratoria* draws "best" examples from an age and rhetor long departed from Quintilian's Rome.

At the end of his account of Cicero's life, Plutarch wrote that when Romans saw what Antony had done by having parts of Cicero's body placed on the Rostra, they felt that they viewed not the demise of a great Republican but the blackness of Antony's own soul. Our lessons from these events can be extended to reinforcing the meaning of *kairos* in Republican Rome. It is clear that rhetoric in Rome functioned well when the society had a public which was empowered to use it fully in the administration of legal and civic affairs. Denied that power, the utility of rhetoric as a social force quickly eroded, although its place in education persisted, most likely because facility in expression was valued intrinsically and for personal advancement. Our retrospective view clearly shows that, despite all the eloquently passionate pleadings, rhetoric could not be effective outside the environment that desired and empowered it. Once that situation was lost, rhetoric could do nothing to re-create that environment.

Situational features of rhetoric were of paramount importance during this period. First, the importance and notion of "audience" must be reconsidered. While an audience is central to rhetoric, an audience is inconsequential if it is not empowered with both the ability to determine validity and the authority to act on the consequences of such judgments. Audience, then, is important only in so far as the environment of Republican Rome permitted its authority. Second, constraints in situations involving rhetoric may be such that they permit no resolution to problems which otherwise could be resolved by discourse. In effect, they provide no context for resolution. Finally, the exigence or problematic conditions which warrant rhetorical discourse may be such that they permit no rhetoric at all. Such was the case in latter years of Cicero's Rome, where political conditions so altered the society that the environment itself was the exigence, and one so inherently problematic that it afforded no opportunity for correction other than by revolution.

Many optimistic Republicans believed that the murder of Caesar would be an act of violence that would reinstate the Republican climate. Instead, it merely initiated another power struggle among another set of dynasts which eventually resulted in the Augustan Principate. While Augustus brought long-sought stability and harmony to Rome and while many Republican civic and legal systems continued in operation, his rule as Emperor illustrated that any degree of free expression enjoyed during his rule would be done at the Emperor's pleasure. Oratorical and literary acts not in favor were censured and, on occasion, resulted in the exile of the author, as happened with Ovid. More importantly, the transformation of Rome from a Republic to an Empire is a vivid illustration of *kairos*. In the case of the Republic, the environment and the situations that evolved in less than one hundred years make a strong case for the position that as powerful as rhetoric may be in a society, it is impotent if the environment will not permit its operation. In the regrettable case of the Republic, it was only by violence and tyranny that any condition was re-stabilized that permitted rhetoric to operate again. The resulting operation, however, was no longer as a source of political power, but more as an educational force entrenched in the curriculum of schools throughout the Empire. It is not by coincidence, as Tacitus suggests, that the demise of the Republic is concurrent with the loss of eloquence. The lesson that cost Cicero his life is that the Roman *kairos* controlled the effect of discourse and not the reverse.

Tacitus, writing within generations following Cicero and the collapse of the Republic, firmly believed that rhetoric functioned best in an environment of power, one in which there was enough strife (40) and uncertainty to kindle the flame of eloquence (36). What is implicit in Tacitus' discussion of eloquence, however, is that discourse was written and uttered in an environment in which it made a difference. In this respect, Tacitus' view was in accord with Cicero's. They believed that their forefathers (*De Officiis* 2. 66) had established civic and legal procedures that would not only carry on public functions but would also stabilize and nurture eloquence in a peaceful climate (*Orator* 140-6). One of the great ironies apparent by viewing Republican rhetoric through *kairos* is that the height of eloquence, particularly the latter years of the Republic, occurs when political and social conditions are most unstable. That is, when the *kairos* was most fragile, when chaotic events from the threat of personal assassination to civil war seemed imminent, the tension of the situation provided the occasion for some of the most brilliant displays of rhetoric. This observation does not temper Cicero's views on the importance of social institutions that permit free expression; rather, it underscores the view that "great" rhetoric occurs when conditions are dire but still afford the opportunity for action to result from discourse. After the stabilization of the government and the institutionalization of rhetoric into the educational curriculum, the *kairos* of rhetoric accordingly stabilized. Following Caesar and Augustus, as we shall see later, virtually every Roman emperor became an imperial sponsor of rhetoric in some respect. The testimony of decrees, the records of history and the evidence of archaeological excavations all bear witness to the sustained support for the stable *kairos* of rhetoric in the Imperial Period, and it is only when the Empire itself decays that rhetoric falters. The nature of rhetoric in the Imperial Period is far different from the rhetoric of Cicero's Republic, but it is through an understanding of *kairos* that we shall be able to see those differences with greater precision. Cicero's rhetoric was used as a legitimate tool of social reform, a vehicle for a social movement. Some Republicans would use rhetoric to argue for revolution, others for modification, still others for a revivalistic re-institution of pristine values. All, however, recognized that rhetoric in operation in the courts and assemblies was a sanctioned vehicle for social change, and the environment of the Republic—as delicate and tenuous as it was—nonetheless invited such discourse as its agent for normalization and regulation. In effect, the Republic itself was the Rostra for rhetoric. With the Empire, that Rostra for social expression was transformed into a library for isolated study, personal growth and erudite introspection. The notable difference, however, was not so much the loss of the individuals who could be eloquent, as Augustus, Tacitus and Quintilian believed, but rather the transformation of *kairos*. More than any other single factor the environment for rhetoric shapes its nature, opportunity and character.

chapter III

When Rhetoric Was Outlawed in Rome
The Censure of Greek Rhetoric and the
Emergence of Roman Declamation

The preceding chapters have shown how Greek rhetoric was introduced to Romans and how the environment of the Roman Republic made rhetoric attractive because it was a source of power. Yet despite these opportunities and conditions, the reception of Greek rhetoric into Roman society was initially opposed, particularly when rhetoric was "taught" in schools. To understand why resistance to rhetoric occurred at a time that is popularly considered to be the dawning of the Golden Age of Republican rhetoric, we need to examine the forces in operation prior to that period. One of our primary sources for this period is Suetonius's *De Rhetoribus*. Men such as Suetonius, born in the dawning of the Roman Empire, were beneficiaries of a culture grounded in rhetorical tradition. By the time of Suetonius's birth (c. 69 A.D.), the role of rhetoric had been drastically altered in Rome.

Gaius Suetonius Tranquillus was an antiquarian and biographer of rhetoric, who was never himself the subject of a biography. He is most famous for his accounts of the twelve Roman emperors, known under the collective title of *De Viris Illustribus*. The few extant remarks on the life of Suetonius and his association with rhetoric come from three sources. First, the remarks of Suetonius himself in his own works (*Divus Augustus* 7; *Gaius Caligula* 19; *Nero* 57; *Otho* 10; *Domitianus* 12; *De Grammaticis* 4); second , the letters of the orator, Pliny the Younger (*Epistulae* i. 18, 24, v. 10;

ix. 34; x. 94); and third, the *Scriptores Historiae Augustae* (i. e.: *Hadrian* 11.3; *Commodus Antonius* 10.2; *Maximus et Balbinus* 4.5; *Probus* 2.7; and *Firmus, Saturninus, Proculus, et Bonosus* 1. 1, 2). The information concerning the early years of Suetonius is particularly sketchy. Suetonius was probably born in Rome at about 69 A.D., a date deduced from his remarks describing himself as a "young man" twenty years after Nero's death (*Nero* 57). It is certain that Suetonius came from a family of moderate social position, that his father was a tribune of equestrian rank (*tribunus angusticlavius*) in the Thirteenth Legion, and that Suetonius was educated when schools of rhetoric flourished in Rome (*Otho* 10). At the time Suetonius was educated, Quintilian received his professional chair of rhetoric, after being brought from Spain by the Emperor Galba the year before (68 A.D.). The *Institutio Oratoria* was published about twenty years later.

There is no extant information on the early education of Suetonius, but he did, according to Pliny the Younger, establish himself as a forensic orator of unknown success (*Epistulae* 1. 18) and became a speech consultant to famous orators (*Epistulae* 9. 34). Suetonius's significance in rhetoric, however, lies not in his ability to speak well but in his ability to record rhetorical history. Roman Emperors Trajan and Hadrian provided Suetonius the opportunity to research the history of Roman rhetoric. Under the reign of Trajan, Suetonius received two secretarial appointments (*a studiis* and *a bibliothecis*) and wrote *De Grammaticis et De Rhetoribus*. Under Hadrian, Suetonius received a third appointment to the imperial secretaryship (*epistularum magister*), affording him complete access to the state archives and the opportunity to write on a spectrum of subjects concerning Roman history (*Scriptores Historiae Augustae: Hadrian* 11.3). After his dismissal by Hadrian in 121 A.D. (*Scriptores Historiae Augustae: Hadrian* 11. 3), the quiet and scholarly Suetonius retired to his research and vanished from public view to the extent that even the date of his death is unknown.

Suetonius deserves a prominent position in the rhetorical tradition of the early Roman Empire. Although *De Rhetoribus* is more the product of an antiquarian than a historian when compared with *Dialogus de Oratoribus* of Tacitus (first century A.D.), it reflects the diligent type of scholarship which earned the praise of his ancient readers from Pliny the Younger (*Epistulae* 1. 24) through the various accounts of the *Scriptores Historiae Augustae* (*Probus* 2.7; *Firmus, Saturnius, Proculus, et Bonosus* 1. 1, 2). So meticulous was Suetonius that Pliny the Younger complained about the painstakingly slow publication rate (*Epistulae* 5. 10). We should, however, be grateful for Suetonius's careful scholarship, for *De Rhetoribus* is the only Latin treatise concerned directly with pre-Ciceronian rhetoricians and provides information on the strong opposition to rhetoric, on the radical changes in the educational system of Rome, and on the influence of rhetoricians who otherwise would have been unknown. In an age of florid rhetoric, Suetonius writes clearly and concisely and establishes himself as one of the last representatives of the Quintilianic scholars concerned with the early foundations of Roman rhetoric.

Suetonius's *De Rhetoribus*: Background and Translation

As a treatise covering the earliest known period of Roman rhetorical history, *De Rhetoribus* literally speaks for itself: no criticisms or reviews in antiquity are known, and modern works do little more than describe its general theme (e.g. Bonner 1969: 80, n. 3; Clarke 1966: 10, n. 1; Duff 507). *De Rhetoribus* was the latter half of a fragmented work concerning both the grammarians and rhetoricians of early Rome (*De Grammaticis et Rhetoribus*), which, in turn, was part of an even more inclusive work on the famous men in Rome's history (*De Viris Illustribus*). *De Rhetoribus* was known through the second century A.D., when it was lost until being rediscovered in Germany by Enoc of Ascoli in the mid-fifteenth century. Other fifteenth-century copies of *De Rhetoribus* have since been collected and collated, out of which the 1963 Teubner edition of the Latin text was produced. Obviously this source is important enough not only to warrant translation but, and of equal value, to provide commentary about the context in which Suetonius writes. The English translation offered here is presented with the primary goal of clarity of historical meaning rather than an approximation of Suetonius's Latin artistry.

> Rhetoric was also introduced into Roman society at about the same time as grammar and, in fact, it is common knowledge that rhetoric was received with even more opposition; at some points it was even prohibited to be practiced. To eliminate any doubt of this I shall submit an ancient Senatus Consultum and an edict of the censors:
>
>> During the consulship of Gaius Fannius Strabo and Marcus Valerius Messalla, Marcus Pomponius the praetor put forth the following proposition to the Senate: "As a result of the

discussions that were undertaken regarding the 'philosophers' and 'rhetoricians' the Senate has reached a consensus on the topic that the praetor Marcus Pomponius should take notice and direct his attention, in any way that would seem in accordance with the State's values and his own official obligations, so that these philosophers and rhetoricians not be allowed at Rome."

After some time had passed, the censors Gnaeus Domitius Ahenobarbus and Lucius Licinius Crassus also published an edict concerning philosophers and rhetoricians:

It has been reported to us that there are men who have instituted a new system of education to the youth that assemble in their school: these men have labeled themselves "Latin rhetoricians." Our young men waste whole days in this pursuit. Our ancestors have already decided what they wished free men to learn and what schools to attend. These new precepts that have emerged transcend the custom and habit of our ancestors and do not please us, nor do they seem morally proper. Therefore, we express our sentiments to those who maintain these rhetorical schools and to those who seem to be making a practice of attending these institutions; it does not please us.

Gradually rhetoric was recognized as both advantageous and honorable, and many sought rhetorical training for both the sake of self-defense and esteem. Cicero himself declaimed in Greek all the way up to his praetorship, and as a rather old man, he even declaimed in Latin with the consuls Hirtius and Pansa whom he called his "students" and "big boys." Certain historians have recorded that Gnaeus Pompeius, just before the Civil War, habitually declaimed so that he could more easily oppose the case of Gaius Curio, a man of sharp logic, who supported Caesar. In the same respect Marcus Antonius, just like Augustus, did not omit his rhetorical practice during the Mutinan War. Emperor Nero also declaimed right into the first year of his rule, and also twice before that in public.

In addition to this, several of the orators actually published their declamations. And, therefore, since men were inspired by this great enthusiasm, a great abundance of teachers and instructors flowed forth, and indeed rhetoric so prospered that some men of disreputable character had advanced into the senatorial order and to the highest offices. But each and every rhetorician lacked

a uniform approach toward teaching oratory, so much so
that every rhetorician drilled his students in a different
way. Further, early rhetoricians were accustomed to
criticize their very stylish witticism through the use of
rhetorical figures, events and narrative fables on the one
hand, and then to expound and develop their orations
more copiously on the other hand. Occasionally,
rhetoricians would translate Greek works and either praise
or blame distinguished men. They would also show certain
principles of common life leading to enjoyment which
would be useful and necessary, and others which would be
ruinous and superfluous. This was often done to
strengthen or diminish the faith in fables: a kind of theme
which the Greeks called "destructive" and "constructive."
Eventually, these exercises became obsolete and were
followed by argumentative deliberation.

The old style arguments were drawn either from
historical accounts, as of course is still occasionally done,
or from a real event, if perhaps any new occurrence had
taken place. Furthermore, these exercises were usually
presented with even the names of the places inserted. At
least this was practiced in the case of the collected and
published orations, from which it may be appropriate to
refer to the works of one or two as an example.

> During the summer time some young men from the city
> landed on the shore when they had come to Ostia. They
> approached some fishermen drawing in their nets and
> agreed that they would buy the catch for a certain amount.
> Many nets were released. They waited for a long time until
> the nets were drawn. When the nets were drawn in, there
> were no fish, but instead a basket of gold sewn shut. The
> young buyers said that the catch was theirs, but the
> fishermen said that it was theirs.

> Once when a slave dealer was drawing out his cargo of
> slaves for sale from a ship at Brundesium, and since he was
> afraid of the customs officers' levies, he placed a gold charm
> and *toga praetexta* on a handsome and extravagant young
> slave. The deception was easily concealed. When they came
> to Rome, however, the affair was discovered, and the boy
> was tried on the grounds that he was made a free man in
> liberty by the will of his lord.

At one time, moreover, the Greeks labeled these
controversies under the title of "synthesis," though they

were soon called "controversies," but were either fictitious or judicial. These distinguished teachers of whom any history is available, were not at all easily ascertained; it is upon these accounts that I shall draw knowledge about the rhetoricians.

Lucius Plotius Gallus, on the subject of this man, Cicero, mentioned the following in a letter to Marcus Titinius:

> I indeed remember back when we were boys and a certain man named Plotius began to teach in Latin. It so happened that students gathered near him since everyone of the most prominent students was drilled by him. For my own part, I was sorry that I was not permitted to do the same thing. Moreover, I was held back by the advice of very learned men who had thought that one's abilities could become better by certain exercises in Greek.

Marcus Caelius, in an oration for his own defense on a charge of assault, asserted that this same Lucius Plotius Gallus—for he lived for a very long time—had composed the case against his own prosecution for Altratinus and without directly stating his name, Caelius called Plotius a "barley bred rhetorician," mocking him as "puffed, light and coarse."

Lucius Voltacilius Pilutus was said to have served as a slave and was actually even a chained door-keeper, as was the ancient custom, until he was freed because of his genius and zeal toward literature and because he wrote a very forceful prosecution for his patron. Then as a teacher of rhetoric, he instructed Gaius Pompeius Magnus and set forth an account of his father, as well as the son, which are contained in several books. Cornelius Nepos thought that of all freed men Lucius Voltacilius Pilutus was the very first to write an unabridged history, which up to that time was customarily written by the most distinguished men.

Marcus Epidius, a noted blackmailer, established an oratorical school and taught, among the number of his pupils, Marcus Antonius and Augustus. One of those students was Cannutius who was once taunted because he sided with Isauricus, a very capable consular, and followed Isauricus's party in managing the state. Cannutius replied to these taunts that he would rather be a student of Isauricus than a dishonest legal trickster like Epidius. This

man Epidius claimed his own descent from Epidius of
Nuceria, who once threw himself headlong into the
fountains of the Sarnus River and after a little while
emerged with golden horns, immediately vanished, and
was instated among the number of the gods.

Sextus Clodius from Sicily was also a teacher of Latin
and Greek oratory, a man of bad sight but sharp tongue
who said he had extricated a pair of eyes during his
friendship with Marcus Antonius, the triumvir. Clodius
said of Antonius's wife Fulvia, who had one cheek which
was rather swollen, that it tempted the point of his pen—
because of this remark Clodius was not held in great favor
by Antonius. Yet, as soon as Antonius became consul,
Clodius received a huge gift which Cicero reproached
Antonius for in his *Philippics* saying:

> Just for a laugh you use a schoolteacher, and by your own
> approval, and that of your fellow drinkers, you have
> appointed a rhetorician and allowed him to say whatever he
> wishes against you; to be sure he is a witty man but it is a
> rather simple matter to speak with wit against you and your
> own cohorts. But how much fee is given to the rhetorician!
> Listen, Senators, listen and realize the blows to our state.
> You allotted two thousand acres of Leontine plains to the
> rhetorician Sextus Clodius, and even tax exempt, so that at
> a great cost, you could be taught to be wise in nothing.

Gaius Albucius Silus of Novaria, while he was
performing his duties as aedile in his native land was, as it
happened, in the process of pronouncing judgment when
he was dragged from the tribunal by his feet by those men
against whom he was publicly sentencing. Indignant at
this, he immediately rushed toward the gate and from
there went to Rome. On the way Gaius Albucius Silus was
admitted into the home of the orator Plancus, who was
about to practice his declamation and had a custom of
calling on someone who would speak first before him.
Albucius undertook this part and so fulfilled his obligation
that he put Plancus to silence, who did not dare to lower
his prestige by a comparison.

But from this event Albucius established a
distinguished reputation and opened a lecture hall. In his
practice Albucius would, after having set forth a debate
topic, begin speaking and just at the point when he
aroused his emotions he would stand up and deliver the

peroration. He would also declaim in varying manner, at first brilliant and adorned and then, so that he would not be continuously considered by all as a "rhetorician," he would speak succinctly and commonly and in all but colloquial terms. Albucius also pled cases. Indeed, he rather infrequently provided service to only those men of the highest distinction, and then he would speak only in the peroration. Afterwards he renounced the Forum, partially because of shame, partially because of fear; for when he was in a certain legal dispute before the *centumviri* he had offered to his opponent, to whom he had made an unrespectful attack on his parents, the right of making an oath—but he did it only as a figure of speech. "Swear by the ashes of your father and mother who had died irreverently," he said, and he made other remarks in this same way. The taunt was accepted by his opponent, and since it was not rejected by the judges, the decision was secured, but not without great ill-will on the part of Albucius. On another occasion, a murder case at Mediolanum, Albucius was defending with the proconsul Lucius Piso presiding. The lictors kept trying to stop the excessive shouts of praise for Albucius and he became so inflamed that, having wept bitterly over the situation of Italy, he said that it was as if Italy were again being reduced into the form of a province. Albucius kept calling Marcus Brutus, whose statue was directly in view, the originator and protector of laws and liberty—he almost paid the penalties. Now, however, as an older man he returned to Novaria, because of the discomfort of an ulcer. He called the people together and made clear the reasons why he had resolved to die, and after a long customary public address, he gave up and abstained from food. . . .

Suetonius's *On Rhetoricians*: A Commentary

Although left as a fragment, Suetonius's *De Rhetoribus* tells us much about the emergence of rhetoric in the Roman Republic and the reasons for its endurance into the Empire. Suetonius makes it clear that the study of grammar and rhetoric are seen as related. In this instance, however, both were initially held in reproach. Yet, their association also makes it clear that the study of writing and oratory were also seen as joined in the early second century B.C., and this unity of orality and literacy would persist for Romans throughout the period. Thus, when Romans discussed expression, much of what is mentioned is applicable to both oral and written communication. The disdain for grammarians and rhetoricians was partly because Rome still closely associated facile expression with Greek culture and viewed the systematic study of speech and writing as a trait of Hellenism. The Roman opposition to both grammar and rhetoric is underscored in Suetonius's *De Grammaticis*. In the beginning passage of this work, Suetonius claims that the humble beginnings of grammar and rhetoric were due in large part to the fact that they were introduced by *"semigraeci"* or Greek Italiotes; in short, the same Greeks that introduced rhetoric to Rome from Magna Graecia. The tension between pristine Roman values of clear, unadorned expression and the obvious advantages of eloquence in a predominantly oral society were the source of great concern to early Romans.

De Rhetoribus makes it clear that patrician opposition to rhetoric being widely taught was due in part to the conservative, aristocratic view that feared an equestrian class empowered by rhetoric. Rising classes who could eloquently express attitudes contrary to patrician interests were a threat. While this view would doubtlessly be an unpopular one to express publicly, the same ends could be attained by the patricians opposing the public teaching of rhetoric on the grounds that it lauded Greek intellectual pursuits and hence fostered an idleness in impractical liberal education that was an antithesis to Roman heritage and culture. Specifically, the opposition to which Suetonius referred in the *De Rhetoribus* is the formal methodology of Greek rhetoric. Throughout the early part of the second century B.C., some Roman patrician circles of education were in strong opposition to the influence of Greek literature on Roman thought (i.e., *Graecomia*). This opposition fostered Roman rhetors such as Cato the Elder, who claimed to be totally ignorant of rhetorical precepts. Their abilities in rhetoric, as Cicero and Quintilian both observed, came from natural skill (Cicero, *Tusculanae Disputationes* 1. 3. 5; Quintilian, *Institutio Oratoria* 9. 4. 4).

The moral tenor of the opposition to rhetoric was not restricted to Greek rhetoric, for Suetonius also makes the patrician view of Latin rhetoric equally clear. The disapproval of Latin rhetoric, however, was registered differently than the *Senatus Consultum* of 161 B.C.. When Latin rhetorical schools were outlawed in 92 B.C. (Tacitus, *Dialogus* 35), the ruling came from the "censors." The censor was a Roman magistrate who had the obligation of controlling and legislating public morals. The edict of a censor carried the weight of a senatorial decree and could legally, in this instance, prohibit rhetoricians from Rome if they were viewed as endangering the morality of the populace. The concept of banning rhetoricians and schools of rhetoric was not unique. Xenophon, as we discussed earlier, reported how the Thirty Tyrants outlawed schools of rhetoric for a brief time in Athens. Moreover, Philodemus indicates that Sparta also prohibited rhetoricians (Philodemus, *Rhetorica* [Sudhaus] I, 14, fr. V; cf. 11, 65, fr. II). In each of these instances the conservative upper class viewed rhetoric as a threat because of its advantages to those who potentially could protest the established hegemony.

We are fortunate to have Suetonius record the names of the censors, Gnaeus Domitius Ahenobarbus and Lucius Licinius Crassus; knowledge about these individuals provides more specific information of the situation. Gnaeus Domitius Ahenobarbus was a descendent from one of the famous Roman patrician families. After his one-year term as consul in 96 B.C. he was soon given the highest religious office, Pontifex Maximus, and was elected as censor with Crassus in 92 B.C. Lucius Licinius Crassus is best known as the spokesman for Cicero in *De Oratore* and as being co-consul again in 95 B.C. with Quintus Scaevola Pontifex. As a strong supporter of a tight aristocratic ruling circle, Crassus advocated *Optimates* policies. Crassus himself, however, was a teacher of oratory to ambitious, aristocratic young Romans. He doubtlessly perceived the influx of new rhetoricians both as a potential challenge to his popularity and as politically empowering. Crassus actually offered a defense of this edict in Cicero's *De Oratore* (3. 24. 93–95), claiming that he prohibited Latin rhetoricians because he thought this mode of instruction would dull, not sharpen the talents of young Romans. It is interesting to note that Gnaeus Domitius Ahenobarbus and Lucius Licinius Crassus shared mutual animosity toward one another (Cicero, *Brutus* 44. 164). One of the few things that they agreed on was this edict banning the teaching of rhetoric.

It is easy to understand support from the conservative Roman Senate for the view of the censors; the senators undoubtedly feared that the influx of rhetoricians could provoke a shift of power from the patrician to the lower classes. A strong precedent for such events occurred in fifth-century B.C. Athens when the popularization of education by sophists helped to shift the power base from the aristocratic *Pentakosiomedimnoi* to the popular *Hoplite* and *Thetes* classes. Roman noblemen recognized that the same imbalance of governmental control that happened in fifth-century B.C. Athens could happen between their own *Optimates* and *Populares* (Taylor).

So obvious was this conservative mentality that Cicero, three decades later, often expressed his awareness that the nobility tried to maintain its collusion in such matters (*In Verrem* v. 70. 180; *Epistulae ad Atticum* 4. 8a).

The Emergence of Roman Declamation

Readers will note how Suetonius comments on the "lack of a unified approach toward teaching." An even more recent contemporary to the emergence of declamation at Rome than Suetonius, Seneca the Elder (c. 54 B.C.–39 A.D.), confirms that earlier declaimers did not even leave copies of their work, let alone a history (*Controversiae* 1. Pref. 11). The lack of a unified method is understandable when one realizes that the unknown author of the *Rhetorica ad Herennium* did not introduce this first Latin textbook of rhetoric until c. 86–82 B.C. Only after the *Rhetorica ad Herennium* does any synthesis appear, beginning with Cicero's *De Inventione*. Up to this time, as Cicero writes, there was "total ignorance of a system" of rhetoric (*De Oratore* 1. 4. 14). Cicero's comments, however, are unduly harsh. Roman political, jurisprudential and ceremonial systems had encouraged effective rhetorical expression since the Republic. While it may well be true that the rigorous systematic study of expression so closely associated with rhetoric was not manifested until the second century B.C., it is nonetheless inaccurate to devalue the important approach to rhetoric taught in the schools of declamation. Seneca the Elder is our best illustration of the early notions of declamation and how its popularity paved the way for rhetoric. By the beginning of the first century B.C. "Greek" based rhetoric of the second century B.C. began to evolve into Latin rhetoric. Seneca mentions that Plotius was the first of the Latin rhetoricians to teach and dates his practice to the childhood of Cicero or the early decades of the first century B.C. (*Controversiae* 2. Pref. 5). Roman declamation also began to be taught by individuals of some status other than freedman. Blandus, whom Seneca mentions as just such a rhetorician, was an *equs* or Roman knight (*Controversiae* 2. Pref. 5). A. Fred Sochatoff (1939) demonstrated how much of the early theory of Seneca's declamation is grounded in principles that would be compatible with later, more abstract Roman rhetorical theory. Intertwined in Seneca's models of declamations are his concern for high ethical standards and his regret over the "current negligence" over the study of memory and history. Care over diction, word choice, order and arrangement all make apparent Seneca's concern over the standards of eloquence. These principles of Seneca's declamation, Sochatoff argues, are "the cardinal tenets upon which his rhetorical system is based and underlie his beliefs not only concerning the practice of oratory . . . but also in regard to related topics of the field" (354). Sochatoff's early work on Roman declamation is well supported by S. F. Bonner, whose later *Roman Declamation in the Late Republic and Early Empire* (1969) provides the sort of meticulous accounting of Seneca's numerous model compositions that Sochatoff was unable to develop within the limits of his article-length study. Sochatoff and Bonner, however, changed forever the way historians of rhetoric would view Roman declamation. Once considered a pedantic, solipsistic exercise, Sochatoff and Bonner's scholarship demonstrates that the intricate, detailed procedures of declamation constituted pragmatic training in the sort of jurisprudential and political modes of expression that sustained Roman education and civilization for centuries (Bonner 1977).

As Suetonius illustrates, even in these early forms of declamations, rhetorical treatises and school exercises, the influence of Greek rhetoric through pedagogues is apparent but not reciprocal. D. A. Russell's statement that "Greeks did not learn from Romans—least of all in rhetoric" is a stern but essentially accurate observation (1983: 3). Seneca, in a fashion typical of early Latin rhetoricians of the Republic, acknowledges Greek rhetoric as the standard and source of practice, but does so in a disparaging tone, referring to Greek rhetoricians as "insolent" (*Controversiae* 1. Pref. 6–7). As we shall discuss later, Romans may have disapproved of some features of Greek rhetoric, but they did not hesitate to adapt and modify those which they liked. The Greek concept of *stasis*— the heuristic process for finding the point at issue in a dispute—is a good illustration of the Roman dismissal (and later appropriation) of features of Greek rhetoric. Much of what we know about declamation comes predominantly from such Roman authors who, according to Russell (3), virtually omitted *stasis* in their work. Such was hardly the case with Greek practitioners, as illustrated by Sopatros and Hermogenes. Russell has, in fact, illustrated that *stasis* was not only a "vital subject" but the theory which served as the "guiding principle" for Greek declamation (7, 41). Later Roman rhetoricians, including those such as Cicero who had been taught rhetoric through declamation, saw *stasis* as important for rhetoric and unhesitatingly appropriated it into their own works under the Latin headings of *constitutio* or *status*. Yet, in both its Greek and Roman forms, declamation was not only oral performance but a literary activity as well. Greek declamation was a lively activity, perhaps even more so than its celebrated Roman counterpart, but the dynamism of oral performance should not detract from the fact that Russell establishes: declamation was a composing process involving both vocal and written heuristics.

Greek and Latin schools of declamation gained widespread popularity in the Republic for a number of reasons. Romans had no concept of public, municipal-supported education. Study beyond the home was the privilege of those wealthy enough to afford it. The study of Greek was so fashionable among Romans of means that they exposed their children to its study—virtually from birth— through Greek slaves (Tacitus, *Dialogus* 29). Schools of declamation also became centers for the advanced study of Greek and Latin literature (Quintilian 1. 4. 1–5). So popular were the schools of Greek and Latin declamation that Quintilian commented that by his time many believed it to be the sole method to become facile in expression (2. 10. 1–4). Closely connected to Quintilian's observation is the second reason for the popularity of Greek and Roman declamation. Many Romans, including Quintilian, saw that the art of writing was closely connected to speaking (1. 4. 1–5) and that such an education was necessary for success in law and politics. Greek and Latin declamation in the Republic offered the practical training that benefited such public careers. Thus we can see that the supply of Greek *paedagogoi* and rhetoricians from southern Italy would find Rome an attractive site where their household services and schools for rhetoric would be in demand for both pragmatic and cultural reasons.

These conditions help to explain the emergence, evolution and popularity of declamation at Rome. Roman declamation was a system of teaching rhetoric through forensic (*controversiae*) and persuasive (*suasoriae*) themes. Young Romans engaged in exercise where they studied model speeches, composed their own orations and engaged in thematic debates (Bonner 1969). Romans such as Seneca the Elder would soon regularize and systematize the study of declamation (Sochatoff 1939) in their own manner. Under Roman declamation, values consistent with Roman morality and culture would be the basis for exercises and thus a system of rhetoric more palatable to pristine-minded Romans than the earlier Greek forms. The declamations that Suetonius offers as illustrations are ones grounded in training in law and politics. At the same time, however, these Roman declamations are presented in an epideictic mode. That is, these exercises trained young Romans in forensic and deliberative argument while, indirectly, teaching them to see the moral values at issue in questions of justice and policy.

Later Latin writers such as Petronius (*Satyricon* 1) would criticize the study of declamation for its excesses. It is also apparent from Suetonius that, at least to some degree, the animosity toward Greek rhetoricians and even the study of rhetoric itself diminished. Rhetoricians, both Greek and Roman, eventually taught prominent Romans, despite the fact that some such as Lucius Plotius Gallus openly allied with the *Optimates* (Cicero, *Pro Archia Poeta* 9. 20). *De Rhetoribus* further makes it clear that rhetoric became tolerable in Rome and eventually fashionable, through declamation. While principles were doubtlessly learned through Greek systems, these methods were adapted to Roman preferences and themes. Training in declamation was a popular and acceptable mode of rhetoric because it not only provided a valuable educational experience for the young but also—because of its epideictic topics—an indirect way of reinforcing Roman values.

A point of major significance in the history of rhetoric can be drawn from the *De Rhetoribus* of Suetonius. Transplanted Greek rhetoric survived the dark ages of the early Roman Republic. In spite of the strong aristocratic attempts to suppress and outlaw rhetoric, many young Romans, some of whom were non-aristocrats, continued to study rhetoric and to gain power in the law courts and eventually in politics. In the orally dominated culture of Rome, a symbiotic relationship emerged between rhetoric and politics. Young Romans studied the art of persuasion from Greek and Roman rhetoricians, rose through minor governmental offices, established their military abilities on the battlefield and their rhetorical ability on the Rostra, and gained strong positions of power in the Senate. In the early years of the Republic, Romans such as Cato the Elder drew their sources of power from their own natural oratorical ability and from their status as members of the landed aristocracy. The *De Rhetoribus*, however, reveals that in the later years of the Roman Republic rhetoric gained importance and became such a strong source of power in Roman politics that Cicero could utilize the forces of rhetoric and by 63 B.C. become the first non-aristocrat (*novus homo*) to be elected consul in approximately three decades. After Cicero, the necessity of rhetoric for political success in the Republic became increasingly essential until the monarchial Principate of Augustus transformed rhetoric from a political to an educational power. By the time Suetonius wrote *De Rhetoribus* the Roman revolution had so altered the study of rhetoric that he viewed it more as an antiquarian, describing a type of rhetoric that had become a curious artifact, an archaic subject far different from the version practiced by his contemporaries in the Empire.

chapter IV

The "Latinization" of Greek Rhetoric
A Revolution of Attitude

As Suetonius's treatise on rhetoric documents, Romans did come to accept not only Greek rhetoric but the "Latinized" Roman version as well. What, in retrospect, can we say accounts for this change of attitude? We know that many Romans admired the laconic values of their ancestors. Quintilian records that Cornelia, the mother of the Gracchi, was directly responsible for the early education of her famous sons (1. 5. 6). Another famous early Roman, Cato the Censor (also called Cato the Elder), claimed that education was a parental obligation and that foreign influences on children were to be avoided if pristine Roman morals were to be preserved (Plutarch, *Cato Maior* 20). In fact, Quintilian believed that Romans had admired a simple, unadorned style of rhetoric even before the Gracchi and Cato (8. 5. 33). If such a view as Cato's is representative of the attitudes of his contemporary Romans, how then do we explain the acceptance and assimilation of Greek rhetoric into Roman culture? The question is an important one, for in seeking an explanation we can gain greater insight into the social realities that accommodated the contradictory values.

Greek *Techne* vs. Roman *Ratio*

While the importance of the family and austere Roman morals so aptly captured in Cato's views were publicly expressed, the realities of history offer a somewhat different picture. Such values, it becomes apparent, were praised but not always practiced. The systematic education of young Romans, certainly beyond childhood, was heavily influenced by Greek practices. As Jerome Carcopino claims, few wealthy, noble Romans were inclined to participate directly in the education of their children (103). For this task, many Romans entrusted their children to Greek servants or *paedagogoi* (Tacitus, *Dialogus* 29). Quintilian strongly believed that systematic study at school was far better than education at home (2. 3. 10) and that Roman children should begin with Greek rather than their native Latin (1. 1. 12). At the time that the child was ready to be educated outside the home, he was entrusted to the *grammaticus*. Here, too, the young student was exposed to Greek education. "The first professors of grammar and rhetoric," Carcopino notes, "whom they permitted to set up in Rome were [Greek] refugees from Asia and Egypt, victims of Aristonicus and of Ptolemy Physkon, to whom Rome offered sanctuary" (108). We know that these Greek teachers were then replaced by the Greek-Italians of Magna Graecia. By the time a young man was ready to leave the *grammaticus* and study under the rhetorician, the emphasis was overwhelmingly Greek both in the systems studied and in the language spoken (Gwynn 34–58). Young Romans were introduced to writing and literature as arts by the *grammaticus*. Here also Quintilian recommends that students should begin with Greek (1. 4. 2). Through the study of Greek, both the *grammaticus* and the rhetorician—working together—instruct in declamation. As mentioned earlier, this training was not only beneficial but possibly unavoidable, since many of these early teachers were (Greek) freedmen (Seneca the Elder, *Controversiae* 2. Pref. 5; Cicero, *Orator* 145). From household servants to esteemed sophists, the emphasis on education was Greek.

The benefits of Greek education in rhetoric and literature were recognized as superior by Romans. As discussed earlier, even Cato the Censor with his rigid views on Roman education was impressed by the benefits of Greek rhetoric (Quintilian, *Institutio Oratoria* 12. 11. 23). An admirer of Demosthenes and familiar with Greek literature, Cato recognized in rhetoric values synonymous with higher education. Plutarch's account of Cato (*Cato Maior*) illustrates the paradox that Romans faced with Greek rhetoric. On the one hand, their desired persona was to preserve educational practices that lauded the Roman ancestral view of deeds over words and fluency through knowledge rather than refinement of expressive skills. Yet, the power of rhetoric in civic functions was all too apparent—and troublesome—leading to the censoring of schools of rhetoric. Romans recognized the merits of the Greek *techne* or system of rhetoric but still desired to develop their own *ratio* or system for Latin rhetoric.

Some Romans not only had strong objections to the teaching of rhetoric, they also had reservations about many of the Greek models held up as standards of eloquence. The technicalities associated with Greek rhetoric, the fact that it was other-than-Roman, and the belief that it could lead to inappropriate excesses and even effusive style were all major points of criticism. Yet, several prominent Romans of the second century B.C. were great admirers of Greek culture and rhetoric. This intellectual fraternity has been retrospectively labeled the Scipionic Circle, after the great Roman general and philhelline, Publius Cornelius Scipio Aemilianus Africanus Numantinus (Cicero, *De Amicitia* 69). George Kennedy clearly reveals the importance of the Scipionic Circle to Roman rhetoric in his work, *The Art of Rhetoric in the Roman World* (60–71). Essentially, these Romans were great admirers of Stoic philosophy and the careful and controlled literary style of the Greek historian Polybius, who became a personal friend of Scipio. Of all the qualities (and faults) of Greek rhetoric, the Scipionic Circle gravitated toward those Hellenic models that stood for clarity and lucidity. Their admiration for Greek education was clear. The Younger Scipio, as Kennedy tell us, was himself the beneficiary of a thorough Greek education (64). Yet, their attraction to the Greek ideal of intellectual excellence or *paideia* was directed toward their own Latin language. The Scipionic Circle saw in Greek education a paradigm which could supply a standard for eloquence in their own tongue. "The Scipionic Circle's greatest contribution to rhetoric and Latin literature," argues Kennedy, "was linguistic consciousness: the introduction of the terms and categories of Greek grammar which could be used in creating and maintaining standards and developing new resources in Latin" (64).

The admiration for Greek systems of rhetoric that favored perspicuity and eloquence through simplicity and directness continued into the first century B.C. As did forerunners of the Scipionic Circle, these Romans admired the plain Attic style of Greek rhetoric and came to be called Roman Atticists. Roman Atticists were well known for their view that the purity of Latin should be maintained against extravagance and foreign influences. As a result, they opposed any form of expression that they considered to be excessive (D'Alton). In the *Brutus*, Cicero cites Calidius and Calvus as two *"urbani"* Atticists who are out-spoken in their views on the correctness of Latin prose artistry or *"Latinitas"* (274, 283). Roman Atticists such as Calvus were quite popular and, according to Quintilian, serious rivals to Cicero (10. 1. 115).

Some may well consider the term "Roman Atticists" ironic, for these pristine Romans often had disparaging remarks to make about Greek rhetoric. They were particularly critical of a form of rhetoric called "Asianism" (e.g. Seneca the Elder, *Controversiae* 1. 2. 22–23), believed to have been the Greek style of rhetoric that came from Asia Minor (Quintilian, *Institutio Oratoria* 12. 10. 16–22). According to Quintilian, the great weakness of practioners of the Asiatic style of rhetoric was their lack of judgment and moderation (8. Pref. 17). Characterizations of Asianism as excessive and even bombastic in the grand style (*Orator*), encouraged the view that any Greek rhetoric other than the simple Attic model was inappropriate and even anti-Roman in character. It appears that the more moderate style of Greek rhetoric, called the Rhodian style, was also subject to criticism by the Roman Atticists (*Brutus*). Roman Atticists correspondingly had a very limited range of tolerance for models of Greek rhetoric. They held the Greek Attic orator and logographer Lysias as their model, since he was known and universally respected for his directness and clarity (*Brutus* 285, 291; *Orator* 28; Quintilian, *Institutio Oratoria* 12. 10. 22). Roman Atticists also criticized colleagues whom they considered to be too ornate and indulging in Greek excesses. Cicero was so accused by Atticists for immoderate rhetorical style; his contemporary, Quintus Hortensius Hortalus, was marked for his ornateness and histrionics as being "Asiatic" (Enos 1988).

While Cicero also had his own reservations about Greek rhetoric and its potential for excess (Enos 1988), he strongly disagreed with the Roman Atticists on their limited range of "acceptable" Greek rhetoric and models. Unlike the Roman Atticists, Cicero stressed the importance of mastering a variety of styles, and even used other Greek models to counter the views of the Roman Atticists. In works such as his *De Oratore*, *Brutus*, and *Orator*, Cicero cites the values of orators such as Demosthenes and educators such as Isocrates to illustrate the range of excellence offered by Greek rhetoric. In making such arguments, Cicero sought to justify his own education and approach to rhetoric. What Cicero also did in the process, however, was make a strong and sustained argument for the inclusiveness of Greek rhetoric into Roman education and culture.

The Pragmatic Value of Declamation: The Route to Law and Politics

Republican Rome was an "oral" society. The means of communication for social and political operation were assemblies where oral discourse could determine policy and shape events. Yet in a real sense Republican Rome was also a literate society. The distinguished authors who would crown the later Augustan Principate were beneficiaries of traditions of patronage established during the Republic. Public reading and recitation were common practices for the publication of civic and cultural matters. In short, the society, while understandably dominated by oral modes of expression, had integrated written discourse, even if its primary function was to facilitate and preserve oral discourse.

Declamation became a source for refining oral and written skills in civic affairs. Quintilian records that Marcus Porcius Latro, the first Latin rhetorician of any distinction, based his teaching of declamation on the assumption that it was a preparation for advocacy (10. 5. 18). Cicero stated in the *Brutus* (305) that as a youth he wrote, recited and composed every day. In his *Tusculanae Disputationes* (1. 7), he noted that he consistently declaimed more forensic orations (*controversiae*) than anyone else. Similar to many other Romans, Cicero continued this childhood practice throughout his legal career. As we saw in the last chapter, Suetonius recorded the consistency with which Cicero declaimed in Greek and Latin throughout his career (*De Rhetoribus* 25). Cicero's ability to read, write, and speak Greek is important for understanding both the source and range of his literacy training, as well as his rhetorical abilities. Being able to read Greek and having Demosthenes as his model for delivery and argument meant that Cicero "read" Demosthenes; that is, Cicero used his literate ability to understand Demosthenes' oratorical qualities. Toward the end of his legal career, Cicero wrote his *De Optimo Genere Oratorum*, which he claims to be a preface to his Latin translation of the speeches of Demosthenes and Aeschines (17–18). Cicero was able to benefit from Demosthenes' oratory in the original Greek and eventually to use his literate skills to try to translate those benefits to his Latin readers. Such skills reveal a harmony between oral discourse and composition, a holistic approach to oral and written expression which Cicero nurtured throughout his career. Cicero's comments also make it apparent that the schools and practice of declamation functioned as literacy centers for young Romans, who continued to refine both their oral and literate skills well into adulthood.

Cicero's training, while intense and long, was not unique. Writing speeches in preparation for oral presentation was popular in both Greece and Rome. Quintilian was fortunate enough to have access to Cicero's notes and mentioned in his *Institutio Oratoria* that Cicero frequently wrote out the most essential portions—particularly the opening remarks—beforehand and then invented subsequent lines of argument at the moment (10. 7. 30–31). Cicero also used writing as a means of recording these spontaneous lines of argument. Plutarch believed that Cicero popularized the Greek method of shorthand composition in Rome and, with his freedman, Tiro, developed a system of tachygraphy that permitted rapid recording of oral discourse (Plutarch, *Vitae Parallelae: Cato Minor* 23). While Cicero was clearly adept at this method of shorthand, Tiro was unquestionably an invaluable aid to his composition (Cicero, *Epistulae ad Familiares* 16. 14, 20 ff). It could be reasonably surmised that Tiro would record Cicero's oral arguments—doubtlessly to capture impromptu passages from the previously composed notes—and have the basic text for a polished composition. Fully persuaded that writing was the greatest aid to effective oratory, Cicero believed that lack of motivation or ability and fear of criticism were the constraints that inhibited most orators from publishing their speeches (*Brutus* 91–93). Obviously, such shortcomings were not concerns for Cicero and other orators who sought notoriety through publication.

Cicero's writings reveal both his own practice in declamation and how other Romans saw declamation as pragmatic. Cicero remarked in his *Brutus* that Appius Claudius Caecus was the first orator he knew to record his oral arguments for posterity (61). The practice of recording fully developed orations for public distribution continued and became common among Romans. Sensitive to the potential effect of his writing, Cicero was concerned about copyists who would draft inferior "pirate" texts. On one occasion Cicero wrote to his friend, Atticus, commenting on a circulating text of one of his speeches which he had neither written nor spoken (*Epistulae ad Atticum* 3. 12)! Cicero, however, revolutionized the custom and used the publication of his oral rhetoric as the opportunity to make social statements. His great talent was in recognizing and mastering legal composition. The route to such mastery was grounded in the oratorical training he had received in Greek and Roman declamation.

Legal training was dominated and driven by proficiency in oral performance. As a young man, Cicero expressed interest in becoming a student of Lucius Plotius Gallus, the famous founder of the first Latin rhetorical school in 95 B.C., but was dissuaded because of Gallus' reputation (see chapter three) as a "barley-inflated" rhetorician, "puffed, light, and coarse" (Suetonius, *De Rhetoribus* 26). Having rejected Gallus, Cicero initiated his training in forensic rhetoric by learning the theoretical intricacies of legal procedure from the younger Quintus Mucius Scaevola and the practical application of legal strategies from Quintus Hortensius Hortalus. Cicero mentioned that his father introduced him to Scaevola, the jurist, with the understanding "that, as long as I could and he permitted, I would never leave the old man's side" (*De Amicitia* 1). Under Scaevola's guidance, Cicero memorized precepts and legal opinions with such commitment that he professed in *De Legibus* that he never seemed to be so absorbed in oratory as to turn away completely from civil law (1. 13; *De Amicitia* 1). For practical experience in the Forum, however, Cicero "followed in the steps of Quintus Hortensius himself" since he "was considered first in pleading" (*Brutus* 307–8).

Declamation clearly played an important role in the training of Romans such as Cicero. Much of the early phase of Cicero's legal preparation stressed observation, imitation and a mentor-apprentice relationship. Such methods are well suited to acquiring proficiency in orally dominated expression and, in fact, are similar to techniques of education for oral composition learned in schools of Greek and Roman declamation. After training in declamation, young Romans observed models outside the classroom, often attaching themselves to prominent individuals as did Cicero in his preparation for a legal career as a route into politics. Observation and imitation are common features in the learning of oral compositional techniques. Bards and rhapsodes frequently learned techniques of oral composition by intense, sustained observation of experts, and Cicero appears to have done much the same in his legal preparation.

Cicero was fortunate enough to enjoy a three-year period during his education where Rome, free from war, provided active courts for young orators to observe (*Brutus* 308). "At that time [81–80 B.C.]," wrote Cicero, "I first began to take private and public cases, not so that I could learn in the Forum, which several of my contemporaries did, but so that I could come into the Forum as educated as possible" (*Brutus* 311). Cicero combined his legal training in the Forum with an emphasis in ethical philosophy, as he mentioned in his *De Natura Deorum*: "I did not begin to study philosophy suddenly or moderately. From my youth, I exhausted effort and care in that discipline, and even when it appeared negligible, I was actually studying philosophy extensively, which my orations, crammed with philosophical maxims, reveal; [as well as] the very learned friends who have always enriched my home, and the professors who gave me instruction—Diodotus, Philo, Antiochus, and Posidonius. In fact, if all the philosophical precepts are relevant to life, I think that I upheld those principles which reason and education dictate, both in my public and private matters" (6–7). When Cicero was very young, the Epicurean Phaedrus taught him philosophy but—as Aubrey Gwynn maintains—made little impression (1926: 69). Yet, during the period after the three-year peace, when Cicero thought the courts had all but vanished, he turned "completely" to Philo, the head of the Academy, as well as to other Greek scholars who fled to Rome because of the Mithridatic War (*Brutus* 306).

We have witnessed how Greek rhetoric was the basis for Latin schools of rhetoric. If Cicero's training is indicative of other prominent Romans, we can see that his desire to continue his studies in rhetoric by going to Greece was an indirect affirmation of Roman recognition of the basis for rhetorical training. At the age of twenty-six, Cicero decided to continue his education abroad after he had spoken in defense of Sextus Roscius in a property dispute with one of Sulla's henchmen, L. Cornelius Chrysogonus. During his two years abroad (79–77 B.C.), Cicero studied in Athens, Asia Minor and Rhodes. He spent the first six months of his foreign studies in Athens, continuing his philosophical education under the *scholarchos* Antiochus, who emphasized the doctrines of the Old Academy (*Brutus* 315). While in Athens, Cicero combined the philosophical education obtained from Antiochus with rhetorical exercises under Demetrius, the Syrian, whom he described as "a long standing and not obscure teacher of oratory" (*Brutus* 315).

In Asia, where the predominant rhetorical tradition emphasized the sort of embellishment criticized by Dionysius of Halicarnassus as "replete with petty artifices, ignoble, [and] nonvirile," Cicero studied under Menippus of Stratonicea, whom he considered "the most eloquently eminent orator in all Asia at the time" (Dionysius of Hallicarnassus, quoted in Sihler 57; *Brutus* 315). Cicero studied under other rhetorical scholars of Asia Minor who are now little more than names to us: Dionysius of Magnesia, Aeschylus of Cnidus, and Xenocles of Adramyttium. One of Cicero's most beneficial experiences, however, came from his education in Rhodes when he studied under Apollonius Molo. Cicero believed Molo's skill as a pleader, logographer, and teacher helped temper his own excessively flamboyant style (*Brutus* 316).

Cicero's Greek education exposed him to two important features of rhetorical instruction which facilitated his ability in the composition of oral argument. His Greek education provided training in logography, exposing him to the process of speech composition that had been refined for about four centuries. Second, Cicero was instructed in Greek declamation, which emphasized different skills than his training in Roman declamation (cf. Russell 1983; Bonner 1969). Roman declamation stressed oral argument; in fact, it was a standard feature of legal training. Greek declamation, which was less accessible to other Roman advocates, stressed written composition skills and actively instituted such principles as *stasis* as part of the exercises. Thus, Cicero had the benefits of logography and Greek declamation to draw on when he composed his orations and had, by his own accounts, benefited greatly from such training in an integrated writing-speaking approach.

Cicero returned to Rome holding strong opinions about the tenets of his rhetorical education, which he hoped to apply to the law courts and his political career. He later expressed these sentiments in *De Oratore*: "Oratory ought to be directed out of this private and cloistral exercise [and] into the pubic mainstream, into the arena, into the clamor, into the camp, and into forensic debate; everything must be employed and risked to the strength of her talent. In short, imprisoned meditation ought to be brought into the light of truth" (1. 157). A survey of Cicero's preparation for civic life demonstrates that whatever natural ability and practical experience he may have possessed was complemented by an uncommonly comprehensive education in such areas as poetry, philosophy, law and literature, as well as a thorough training in rhetoric and oratory. After his training, Cicero (as did many ambitious young Romans) sought political power through a uniform progression of elected offices or *cursus honorum*: questorship, praetorship, consulship, and censorship. Whether a young Roman was a *nobilis*, whose admission to the Senate was assured by his heritage, or a municipal *novus homo* ("new man"), as was Cicero, the acquisition of strong support was essential for any appreciable degree of political success. Cicero acquired support by offering his services in forensic oratory, establishing a network of influential patrons, clients and friends who provided the necessary support.

Greek Contributions to Roman Orality and Literacy

As mentioned earlier, Rome increasingly became a literate society during the latter years of the Republic. The use of writing grew in virtually every civic function. When the entrusting of laws moved from being orally "preserved" by the patrician class to being publicly inscribed, they not only stabilized the discourse but de-centered the power of interpretation. When Romans began the practice of publishing their speeches, they expanded the audiences from those physically present to an entire Republic (Enos 1988). Concurrent with the rise of Roman literacy was the emergence of their historiography. Gwynn calls the Roman historian Asinius Pollio "the most outstanding literary figure of his generation" and "the direct inheritor of Cicero's literary traditions" (127). Asinius Pollio, Seneca the Elder writes, was the first Roman to begin the practice of declaiming his written compositions to selected listeners (*Controversiae* 4. Pref. 2). In fact, it was the same Asinius Pollio who helped to complete the first State Library in Rome begun by Caesar (Carcopino 193). Perhaps most apparent of all signs of the impact of literacy was the practice of patronage. Here, too, the Romans continued in the Greek tradition of patronage of writers. As Barbara Gold observes, Romans took on the Greek social and political institution of patronage to such a degree in the first century B.C. that it became nothing less than "a literary phenomenon" (67). In each of these instances, the application of rhetoric played an important role in the transformation from an oral to a literate culture.

Greek rhetoric provided a system for facilitating oral and written expression, and the immediate benefits attained by students from schools of declamation reinforced this *techne*. The impact that schools of declamation had on the teaching of writing is particularly important to the development of literacy in the Republic. Schools of declamation initially taught writing as an aid to oral expression, which dominated as the primary mode of communication. Yet, many of the principles of rhetoric taught in these schools facilitate literacy. As writing became important for its own sake, those principles of expression that were seen as helpful in written expression were emphasized. One of the best ways to understand how these important developments of Latin rhetoric through Greek *technai* affect literacy is to see it as a manifestation of *letteraturizzazione*. In his book, *Classical Rhetoric and Its Christian and Secular Tradition from Ancient to Modern Times* (1980), George Kennedy discussed *letteraturizzazione* as a way of explaining how some societies facilitate the transition from orality to literacy by modifying primary principles of oral rhetoric to writing. That is, those techniques of rhetoric that were intended for oral discourse, but are also appropriate to writing, are "literized" into a secondary rhetoric, a rhetoric intended to provide a system to facilitate written expression (Enos and Ackerman 1991). In ancient Greece, the systems of rhetoric that were appropriate to oral communication were modified to include writing. In the Roman Republic, this same sort of phenomenon took place. The systems of Greek rhetoric were seen as valuable both for providing a standard for Roman oratory and for Roman literacy as well. This view becomes even clearer when we recall that both Greeks and Romans viewed inscribed "speeches" as literature and saw the compatibility between oral and written expression in much closer ways than we presently do. From this perspective, the process of *letteraturizzazione* is two-fold: the transferal of principles of Greek rhetoric to Latin and the appropriation of orally-based systems of Greek rhetoric to written Latin prose.

The systems of rhetoric offered by Greek educators were understandably the basis upon which the Romans would develop their own "Latinized" theory. We know that by Cicero's time the heavy emphasis in Greek rhetoric was being transformed to Latin. Naturalized Latin treatises on the Greek art of rhetoric, as Harry Caplan notes, were known to be in circulation as early as the time of the Gracchi (*Of Eloquence* 1), that is, during the latter decades of the second century B.C. Cato, Antonius, and other Roman writers wrote rhetoric manuals, but the best evidence we have is only preserved in extant fragments (Caplan; see Malcovati). The first complete Latin manual of rhetoric, the *Rhetorica ad Herennium*, dates from the early decades of the first century B.C. With our understanding of the historical forces that shaped the reception of rhetoric in Rome, it is clear why Harry Caplan calls this "oldest Latin Art preserved entire" a work best understood as "a Greek art in Latin dress, combining a Roman spirit with Greek doctrine" (1).

Works such as the *Rhetorica ad Herennium*, and Cicero's youthful *De Inventione* (c. 86 B.C.) for that matter, are the consequence of the Roman acceptance of Greek rhetoric. In a certain respect, these early Roman works of rhetoric are Latin versions of Greek rhetoric. In a relatively short period of time, works such as Cicero's *De Oratore* (55 B.C.) are based on Latin models and Roman concerns, which signals a passage into their own rhetoric. The flowering of this Latinized rhetoric, first evident in the corpus of Cicero's later works, is evident in Quintilian's first century A.D. treatise, the *Institutio Oratoria* (c. 94–95). As with Cicero, Quintilian was familiar with Greek concepts, theoreticians and models. Both Cicero and Quintilian use—rather than mimic—Greek theory in the process of articulating their own views on rhetoric. It should be remembered, however, that the Republic of Cicero was not the Empire of Quintilian, and the transformation of Roman society parallels the changes in rhetoric. Seneca the Elder, for example, saw a sharp contrast between the declamation of his contemporaries (c. 37 A.D.) and his youth (born in c. 55 B.C.) Seneca saw earlier declamation as agonistic and combative, comparable to the gladiators fighting in the arena (*Controversiae* 3. Pref. 13). By contrast, one need only read the opening remarks of his *Controversiae* to see the contempt Seneca has both for the undisciplined habits of the youth and the pedantic practices of their teachers of declamation.

Cicero's indebtedness to Greek rhetoric has already been amply illustrated. Quintilian, for example, believed that Cicero committed himself totally to the imitation of such Greeks as Demosthenes, Plato and Isocrates (10. 1. 108–109). Despite the familiarity and use of Greek rhetoric in preparation for his civic life and the high regard he expresses for Greek rhetoricians in his theoretical works, Cicero had clear reservations about Greek rhetoric, illustrating well the curious views Roman Republicans had of Greek-based rhetorical theory and effective Roman advocacy. As a theorist, Cicero was the most influential rhetorician in the history of the Latin-speaking West. His own training in Greek rhetoric from 79–77 B.C. in Athens, Asia Minor and Rhodes shaped his opinions about formal training in the discipline and its application in the civic affairs of Rome. Cicero's praise of Greek rhetoricians, however, was selective. He lauded the type of Athenian rhetoric which he saw in Plato's argumentation but believed that many contemporary "Greeklings" sought controversy more than truth (*De Oratore* 1. 47). Excluding the teachers under whom he studied as a young man, Cicero rarely praised any rhetorician—let alone a Greek rhetorician—in public and never while pleading in the courts (Enos 1988: 79). His praise was limited for the most part to early Greek orators such as Demosthenes and Aeschines, primarily because they were men who used oratory for the benefit of the State (*De Optimo Genere Oratorum* 20–23). Cicero also had little use for sophistic pedantry, as is reflected in his *De Oratore* when Crassus—taking Sulpicius's question as to whether rhetoric was an "art" as a personal affront—asks if he ought to be considered "some sort of leisurely, jabbering, present-day Greekling, who is perhaps learned and educated" (1. 102). Later in the dialogue, Catulus, discussing the necessity of practice, argues that he does "not need the help of some Greek teacher, who chants very common maxims to me when he himself has never looked upon the Forum or any law court" (2. 75). Cicero's criticism of foppish rhetoric was not limited to the Greeks; in fact, the lack of practicality in schoolbook rhetorical exercises so annoyed Cicero that he even rejected his own *De Inventione* as the pedantic "notebook" of a boy (*De Oratore* 1. 5).

Our understanding of Cicero's mixed attitude toward Greek rhetoric needs to be tempered with the times. In the Republic of Cicero, rhetoric was a source of civic power. Always the pragmatist in oral argument, Cicero would condemn in public argument even those whom he lauded in his theoretical works, if he felt that it bettered his cause. In fact, it is apparent in at least two of his orations, the *Pro Cluentio* and the *Pro Scauro*, that Cicero was not above making prejudicial remarks against Greeks, Jews and Sardinians in an effort to discredit their testimony. Yet, rather than focusing on isolated statements, certain values become apparent if viewed over his life. Cicero had a high regard for Greek rhetoric, he saw it as a tool that prepared him well for the responsibilities of civic life. As a theoretician, Cicero fashioned his own rhetoric but acknowledged his indebtedness to Greek thinkers. When rhetoric changed from a tool of power in the Republic to a source of education in the Empire, however, the perspective on Greek rhetoric evidenced by Cicero also changed—as is illustrated by the views of Quintilian.

While Cicero was the premiere advocate of the Republic, Quintilian was the preeminent educator of the Empire, and his orientation reflects his different view on Greek rhetoric. We have already seen how Quintilian strongly advocated the study of Greek literature and rhetoric as a primary aspect of the education of young Romans. In fact, his *Institutio Oratoria* shows that he was much more receptive to assimilating Greek rhetoric than characterized by some scholars (e.g. D'Alton). Books II and III of the *Institutio Oratoria* demonstrate Quintilian's intimate knowledge of Greek rhetoric's history and theory. He acknowledges, for example, that his belief in the study of rhetoric through models comes from Greek practice (2. 5. 1–3, 23). The other books of the *Institutio Oratoria* demonstrate further the range and depth of his knowledge of Greek rhetoric and how easily he incorporates its important features into his own work. Book IV shows Quintilian's knowledge of Greek theories of arrangement, while Book V is a discussion of Greek concepts of proof, probability and comparison. Quintilian devotes part of Book VI to a discussion of the Greek concept of ethos, for which he feels no Latin equivalent exists (6. 2. 8). His discussion, however, is a good illustration of his knowledge of the technical features of Greek rhetoric. Quintilian, as he often does with other technical terms of Greek rhetoric, first introduces the concept in Greek and then seeks to provide a corresponding or equivalent Latin term. In this instance, Quintilian positions ethos with another form of artistic proof, pathos (e.g. 6. 2. 8–20). While Quintilian's interpretation of ethos may not conform to our current views (Enos and Schnakenberg), his command of Greek rhetoric is clearly demonstrated.

Quintilian's use of Greek rhetoric shows that he does not merely translate Greek rhetoric into Latin but transfers and adapts it to serve his own theory. Book VII, where Quintilian discusses the arrangement and nature of argument, is a good illustration of his use of Greek rhetorical theory. Quintilian will often cite technical Greek terms in the original Greek (e.g. 7. 4. 7–16). In his discussion, Quintilian uses Greek concepts as a way of making a comparison or drawing a contrast with its Latin equivalent. Here Greek rhetoric is used not with dependency but either as a point of comparison or to note a curiosity. The same practice is also done in his discussion of tropes in Book VIII and figures in Book IX. Quintilian's use of Greek rhetoric differs greatly from the educators who preceded Cicero in the Republic. In this respect, it is apparent that Quintilian has refined the process begun by Cicero of adapting Greek rhetoric into a now stabilized, identifiable Latin rhetoric. Quintilian acknowledges that Latin rhetoric was a "disciple" to Greek rhetoric (12. 10. 27). It is also possible (and perhaps more accurate) to infer that Quintilian often compares Greeks with Romans both to show how close Romans are to Greeks in the language arts and, in some instances, how Romans have surpassed them (e.g. 10. 1. 93–109, 123). Regardless of intent, however, his use and command of Greek rhetoric is well demonstrated.

To help understand this transformation in the Roman revolution from Republic to Empire, it is necessary to understand why rhetoric was seen as valuable both within the Republic and later within the Empire. Greek rhetoricians contributed indirectly toward the development of Roman rhetoric by providing well established systems that facilitated both the oral and written expression of Latin prose artistry. By the time of Julius Caesar— and certainly by the time of Augustus—fluency in Greek prose was valued by many prominent Romans as a sign of cultural refinement. Cicero, Quintilian and (his contemporary) Pliny the Younger, advocated that students alternate translating passages from Greek into Latin to develop fluency (Cicero, *De Oratore* 1. 155; Quintilian, *Institutio Oratoria* 10. 5. 2–3; Pliny the Younger, *Epistulae* 7. 9. 2; Lundy and Thompson 411). We should not forget, however, that while Greek rhetoricians were valued for what they contributed to Roman rhetoric, they also continued to advance contributions in their own language; here too Roman support is apparent. Under the auspices of such support from prominent Romans, Greek rhetoric flourished.

As indicated in the beginning of this study, our concern here is with the impact that Greek rhetoric had on Roman culture and not with specific theoretical advancements. It is important to note, however, that Greek sophists flourished under Roman rule throughout the Empire and that several fine works have recorded the particulars of this phenomenon. G.W. Bowersock's *Greek Sophists in the Roman Empire* is the most well known for dealing with the details of this topic, and Cecil W. Wooten provides an excellent translation of one of the most prominent of these Greek thinkers in *Hermogenes' On Types of Style*. Those wishing to read about the specific contributions made by Greek rhetoricians in the late Republic and Empire are encouraged to consult George Kennedy's *The Art of Rhetoric in the Roman World* and Thomas Conley's *Rhetoric in the European Tradition*. Kennedy's discussion of Dionysius of Halicarnassus, one of several Greek contributors he treats particularly well, provides an excellent overview. Kennedy's treatment is also an excellent prelude to his subsequent work, *Greek Rhetoric Under Christian Emperors*, although that work takes us beyond the scope of our subject.

Our purpose here is to observe what the contributions of Greek sophists tell us about their place in Roman culture. Much of the emphasis of Greek rhetoric under Roman rule dealt with the aesthetic features of expression. Dionysius of Halicarnassus (fl. 30 B.C.), for example, devoted much of his work to establishing standards of criticism and examining the nature of eloquence. In a similar respect, George Kennedy considers the first century A.D. work, Longinus's *On the Sublime*, to be "the most sensitive piece of literary criticism surviving from Antiquity" (369). Dionysius of Halicarnassus, Longinus and scores of other prominent Greek rhetoricians do share traits important to our work. First, the fact that Greek intellectuals thrived under Roman rule—some such as Herodes Atticus even attained high political office and immense wealth—says much about the support they received from Romans. Second, Greek sophists of the Empire placed a far different emphasis on style than did their predecessors during the Republic. Greek sophists of the Republic taught rhetoric with an emphasis on its civic functions—that is, rhetoric as a source of power. Greek rhetoricians of the Empire stressed the grace and refinement of oral and written prose. Under the auspices of the Empire, Greek declamation was less a preparation for agonistic verbal battles and more a source of artistic expression and cultural refinement.

The parallels of Greek rhetoric are captured well in the disposition of the two Sophistics. As we know from the opening section of this book, Greek rhetoricians during the classical period of democratic Athens taught rhetoric as a source of power, a condition which was compatible in many ways with the political climate of Roman Republicanism. As we shall see, the revival of Greek rhetoric in the Second Sophistic of the Empire used the sophists of the First Sophistic as models of eloquence. Their role as standards of eloquence, however, was not for political *dunamis*—except as it operated under the pleasure of Roman officials, such as in ceremonial or epideictic forms. Latin rhetoric, modifying systems of Greek rhetoric for its own ends, also transferred its function from political to educational and stylistic objectives with the change from Republic to Empire. The far different characteristics separating the First from the Second Sophistic illustrate that Greek rhetoric, even while maintaining its focus on Greek discourse, also modified its emphasis from political matters to concerns of diction, syntax, mimesis and criticism. Thus, both the Latinized versions of Greek rhetoric and the Greek rhetoric that maintained its Hellenic character changed due to differing political climates. In both instances these modifications stressed artistic features and literary refinement. As we shall see in the next chapter, the impact on Greek rhetoric by Romans of the Empire is evident in ways other than the support of prominent individual Greek sophists. Roman patronage has a variety of dimensions and in exploring them we have a better insight into the role Greek rhetoric played in the Empire.

Conclusion

Debates about Greek rhetoric are (admittedly) internal to Romans. That is, their disputes are not so much about Greek rhetoric directly but the Roman perception of the appropriateness of Greek rhetoric. Yet, they do tell us much indirectly about the impact of Greek rhetoric and declamation. The Roman interest in Greek models illustrates how seriously they took schools of declamation and how sensitive they were to the impact that Greek rhetoric had on Roman rhetoric and even on Roman culture. The impact of Greek rhetorical theory on Roman rhetoric is evident in several respects. Many of the concepts, taxonomical and classifi-catory systems, and Greek terms appear in Roman manuals. The most striking examples of these Hellenistic residues are in the *Rhetorica ad Herennium* and throughout the corpus of Cicero's own *Rhetorica*. Romans saw features in the theories, systems and models of Greek rhetoric that, when appropriated into Latin, would (they believed) surpass the original Hellenic ideals. It is apparent that rhetoric was viewed as a source of influence and power. The power of this education was in part taken so seriously because its political impact in the Republic was obvious. Yet, after rhetoric diminished as a source of political power with the change from Republic to Empire, its influence persisted. For far different reasons, and in very clear and enduring ways, Roman approval and assimilation of Greek rhetoric manifested itself in support and patronage.

Almost every prominent statesman of the late Republic had been a student of rhetoric. Marcus Antonius, Julius Caesar, Gaius Pompeius Magnus, Quintus Hortensius Hortalus and Marcus Tullius Cicero all varied in their political practices and party politics during the first century B.C. Republic—but all studied rhetoric as a central subject of their education. Although the Roman love for military heroes provided the most expedient path to political success, the ideal Roman leader sought eloquence as well as military prowess to project the desired political image, *dignitas.* Only a Julius Caesar or Augustus could excel in both military and verbal battles, but many a Roman lacking the heart, character or wealth for military life attained marked political success on the strength of rhetorical skill. For these men, the path of political success extended from the feet of the rhetorician to the Rostra, a path followed by a statesman of no less eminence than Marcus Tullius Cicero. Indeed, rhetoric survived and blossomed in the Republic in part because it was a primary source of power for political success. In a society where the only effective form of mass communication was oral, rhetoric—the art of "the good man speaking well"—was imperative.

When Augustus gained complete control of the Roman State and established his Principate in 23 B.C., he created an autocracy which de-emphasized—if not eliminated—the need for rhetoric as a political tool. Although rhetoric waned as a source for attaining political power, it continued to flourish as the dominant emphasis of the educational system of the Empire. Augustus recognized that rhetoric under the control of the State could foster an educational system which would help to resurrect Rome from the corruption, bribery and civil war of the previous one hundred years. The central reason for the success of rhetoric in the Augustan Empire was that it emerged as part of the only educational system which the Romans knew; to deny rhetoric would be synonymous with denying the cultural and intellectual ideals of the Roman State. The rhetorical education which once functioned to mold lawyers and politicians had emerged as the central focus of education itself, and as education became important for its own sake so also did rhetoric.

Recognizing the aesthetic features of Greek literary arts, Romans also encouraged the study of Greek rhetoric for its own sake. Under Roman auspices, individual sophists, and the Second Sophistic itself, flourished.

Romans also cultivated the literary arts in their own language as well. In some instances, these literary achievements had rhetorical ends that served those in authority. Out of this educational system men of letters were produced who could be used as state propagandists for the emperor. Virgil's *Aeneid*, Horace's *Roman Odes*, and Livy's *Ab Urbe Condita* all illustrate how men once educated in rhetoric utilized their literary skills under the imperial patronage of Augustus to popularize the emperor's attempts at cultural and spiritual regeneration. Patronage, both in Greek and Latin rhetoric, not only rewarded aesthetic excellence but the "proper" epideictic praise for those in positions of authority. To best understand this rhetorical dimension of patronage, and especially how it functioned in terms of Greek rhetoric, we need also to examine how Romans manifested patronage in ways other than through benefications to individuals.

chapter V

The Effects of the Roman Revolution on the Rhetorical Tradition of Athens and the Second Sophistic

In the midst of the Peloponnesian War (431–404 B.C.), Pericles took time to honor the Athenian dead by glorifying their city as a cultural center for all Hellas (Thucydides 1. 2. 41). The legacy of Pericles' generation established Athens as the educational center for the study of rhetoric, a tradition which endured for centuries and was recognized throughout Western civilization. Athens' preeminence in rhetorical studies was particularly evident from the second to the fourth Christian centuries, commonly labeled the Athenian Second Sophistic. The prominence which Athens enjoyed during this period has been recognized as early as the writings of Philostratus, and the leadership which Athens exhibited over other educational centers continues to be acknowledged by contemporary researchers (Philostratus, *Vitae Sophistarum* 535; Bowersock 1966: 17 ff.) Even though most scholars recognize that influential Romans considered Athens to be the intellectual center for rhetoric in the Empire and granted "privileges" to her sophists, little is actually known about the relationship between Roman patronage and the intellectual movement in Athens. As a consequence, the nature of an interaction which was critical to the survival of rhetorical studies at Athens has been unexamined.

Because the relationship between Roman patronage and Athenian rhetoric during the Second Sophistic has not been thoroughly treated, a number of misunderstandings have arisen. M.L. Clarke (1971: 131) claims and Donald Lemen Clark (1966: 264–65) implies, for example, that the Second Sophistic was a Greek occurrence, while Aubrey Gwynn (1926: 34–58) and H.I. Marrou (1958: 242–54) stress Greek influences on Roman culture. Other scholars, such as Charles Sears Baldwin (1959: 1–50), limit themselves to examining the prominent individuals and concepts of the Second Sophistic and fundamentally ignore the historical and cultural implications of the movement. Lastly, George Kennedy, in *The Art of Persuasion in Greece*, indicates the need to study the Second Sophistic within the Roman Empire (336); his subsequent work, *The Art of Rhetoric in the Roman World*, provides helpful but limited remarks (e.g., 565–66). In substance, the most influential works on classical rhetoric neglect to treat the effects of Roman patronage upon rhetorical studies at Athens. This cultural interaction had significant influence on the history of rhetoric.

Roman Sponsorship of Athenian Sophists

The emphasis on the role of Athenian educators and their impact ignores the contributions which the Latin West made to support Athens during the Second Sophistic, often relegating Roman participation to the passive role of a fortuitous beneficiary. Yet, more than any other factor, Roman patronage helped create an environment at Athens in which rhetoric and rhetoricians could flourish. The support for the Athenian Second Sophistic came predominantly from the patronage of wealthy Roman families. The effects of this patronage upon the rhetorical tradition of Athens have been partially examined through literary evidence. The endowments by philhellenic Romans, however, extended beyond the patronage of individual sophists and included building programs that would enhance the educational climate of Athens and perpetuate her cultural legacy.

The Roman development of Athens as the cultural center for rhetoric in the Empire was evident even during the Republic. Although the Second Sophistic came into full force in Athens in the second century A.D., the city had long been recognized by Romans as a center for instruction in rhetoric. Sulla's defeat of Mithridates in 86 B.C. resulted in severe destruction to Athens and the decimation of the civic center, the Agora (Pausanias 1. 20. 4–7; McDonald 60–61). Within one generation, however, Athens revived to continue her role as the educational center of rhetoric, and wealthy young Romans such as Cicero came to receive instruction (*Brutus* 2. 315). In fact, Cicero even claimed in his *De Oratore* that the popularity which rhetoric enjoyed in Rome could be directly attributed to its Greek heritage (1. 14). By the second half of the first century B.C., the value of such rhetoricians and educators in liberal arts was clearly recognized by influential Romans. Julius Caesar granted citizenship to liberal arts teachers at Rome, and Augustus extended a range of privileges in the form of honorific immunities to sophists throughout the Empire (Suetonius, *De Viris Illustribus: Divus Augustus* 42, 59; *De Grammaticis 17*). Moreover, as G. W. Bowersock maintains, Antony's defeat at Actium saved Greco-Roman culture, for the intercourse between Greeks and Romans under the Augustine Principate "not only affected the course of Greek literature and rhetoric; it unified East and West" (1966: 122–23). There is little doubt that Augustus believed the fusion of Greco-Roman cultures to be valuable and incorporated "intelligent and loyal Greeks both in his court at Rome and in the Greek-speaking portions of the empire" (1966: 41).

Following the tradition of Caesar and Augustus, emperors (particularly the Flavians) and wealthy Romans adopted the role of educational patrons to sophists throughout the Empire, particularly in Athens. Vespasian (69–79 A.D.), who instituted chairs of rhetoric in Rome at a public stipend, conferred special privileges upon grammarians and orators and established an imperial patronage at an annual stipend of one hundred thousand sesterces for Roman and Greek rhetoricians (Suetonius, *De Viris Illustribus: Divus Vespasianus* 17, 18). It was during this period of educational growth that Quintilian, under the patronage of Vespasian, Titus (79–81 A.D.), and Domitian (81–96 A.D.), prospered and became the first known, imperial endowed professor of rhetoric. In addition to his patronage of Quintilian, Domitian sponsored rhetorical contests and the reconstruction of libraries (Suetonius, *De Viris Illustribus: Domitianus* 4, 13, 20). Roman patronage of sophists continued under the reign of Trajan (98–117 A.D.), who advanced educational programs for the poor (Pliny the Younger, *Panegyricus* 26–28; Philostratus, *Vitae Sophistarum* 532). The zenith of sophistic patronage, however, came with Hadrian (117–138 A.D.). Besides conferring a retirement pension for elderly professors, Hadrian became an ardent proponent of local education throughout the Empire, especially in Athens, where chairs of rhetoric were supported (Pausanias 1. 20. 7; *Scriptores Historiae Augustae: De Vita Hadriani* 15, 16). Hadrian's influence is seen in his immediate successor, Antoninus Pius (138–161 A.D.), who continued to grant privileges to professors of rhetoric and philosophy throughout the Empire (*Scriptores Historiae Augustae: Antoninus Pius* 11).

Patronage became an assumed duty of the emperor by the reign of Marcus Aurelius (161–180), who established an imperial chair of rhetoric and four chairs of philosophy at Athens (Lucian, *Eunuchus* 3; Philostratus, *Vitae Sophistarum* 566, 567). By a careful examination of inscriptions and literary evidence, I. Avotins (1975) has discovered that the imperial chair of rhetoric at Athens was directly established by the emperor about 174 (314–15). This imperial chair of rhetoric was conjoined with a previously established municipal chair of rhetoric, which was salaried by the city and probably available only to Athenian-born sophists (318–19). Although evidence is fragmentary, it does reveal that patronage to the imperial chair of rhetoric was consistent from 174 to 220, with no less than seven sophists receiving support and imperial immunities (324). Although evidence of imperial patronage for rhetoricians indicates that support lasted through the reign of Julian (360–363), the influence of Christian leaders opposing pagan sophism continued to increase (Eunapius, *Vitae Sophistarum* 473, 493). The final gasp of imperial patronage ended in the reign of the Christian emperor Justinian (527–565 A. D.), whose edict in 529 closed the pagan University of Athens and terminated any remaining sophistic influence.

The support Rome extended to sophists was mutually beneficial. At the height of Roman patronage, men of letters used training in rhetoric to advance their public careers by securing the favor of the imperial court through their declamations. Evidence of the rise of sophists in the Roman Empire occurs throughout Eunapius's *Vitae Sophistarum*. Emperor Constans, for example, awarded the sophist Prohaeresius a bronze statue entitled, "Rome, the Queen of Cities, [Presents This] to the King of Oratory" (*Vitae Sophistarum* 492). In order to acquire such magisterial skills of eloquence, eager students gravitated to educational centers such as Athens. The most prominent example of this type of public orator and scholar was Aelius Aristides (c. 117–189). Despite his criticism of sophists, Aristides was taught Greek literature by Alexander of Cotiaeon and studied rhetoric at Athens, possibly under the direction of Herodes Atticus (Aelius Aristides, *Sacred Tales* 5. 38–41). Although Aristides claimed to admire rhetoric for its own sake, he twice went to Rome in an effort to advance his career by public declamations (Behr 1968: 23, 88–90, 103). In fact, one of his most famous orations, "To Rome," was a laudatory account of Roman accomplishments, particularly the administrative policies that incorporate the *Pax Romana* (Aelius Aristides, *Sacred Tales* passim; Behr 1968: 103). Aristides' career, and his own comments, indicate the influence rhetoric could have in securing advancement by attracting imperial power and patronage (Behr 1968: 103). Furthermore, as Aristides himself acknowledged, the center for rhetorical education was Athens (*Panathenaikos* 397). Under this system of reciprocity, Roman patronage helped support Athenian-trained spokesmen similar to Aristides, who could use their ability to serve the Empire.

Roman Sponsorship of Cultural Building Programs

Although sponsorship of individual sophists was extensive, the nature of Roman patronage is incomplete without attention to the cultural building programs directed by Romans at sites such as Athens. The substance of this information is relatively new to classical scholarship, since excavation of the Athenian Agora and "Roman" Athens were not even begun until the 1930s (*The Athenian Agora*). The physical evidence which has come to light through archaeological investigations is largely the product of twentieth-century effort, which means that systematic recording and publication of this research has been done only within the last several decades. The continuing discoveries add a dimension to our knowledge which had previously been restricted to fragmented literary and historical references.

Imperial patronage for the Athenian Second Sophistic, which spanned almost four centuries, reached its height in the second and third Christian centuries, particularly under the reign of Hadrian, and directly paralleled the height of the Athenian Second Sophistic itself. Such a correlation adds new support to the argument that the Athenian Second Sophistic owed its existence to Roman patrons. In order to acquire a more precise view of the rhetorical and educational climate of the Athenian Second Sophistic, the literary evidence must be conjoined with epigraphical and archaeological accounts. In short, the transmitted texts of ancient writers must be complemented by physical evidence which comes from the study of ancient inscriptions and material remains.

Although evidence of the use of the Athenian Agora as a center of civic activity, possibly including education, can be dated epigraphically to at least the sixth century B.C., there is attested physical evidence to indicate that the educational climate attained its fullest development during the period of Roman rule (McDonald 1943: 37–43). In fact, a clear interpretation of Pausanias's account

Permission granted by the American School of Classical Studies at Athens: Agora Excavations.

of the Agora makes apparent the extent of Roman patronage to the cultural building program of Athens (Vanderpool 1949: 128–37). Prior to the period of Roman domination, the sites for oratory and education centered not only in the Agora, where large wooden grandstands (*ikria*) were constructed to accommodate listeners, but also the Boule, Theatre of Dionysius, and the Pnyx (McDonald 1943: 42–44, 46, 55, 59–61; Rhodes 1972). There is strong evidence to indicate, however, that the Bema, or speaker's platform, which functioned as the equivalent to the Roman Rostra, was not even popularized until Roman influence (McDonald 1943: 84–86). In fact, references to the Bema are rare in literature prior to the Romans, who included this construction in their cultural building programs (Athenaeus, *Dipnosophistae* 5. 212e; McDonald 1943: 84, n. 156).

Prior to the Roman influence of the Second Sophistic, these public buildings functioned primarily as meeting places where a democratic climate dominated and where rhetoric was a source of political power. The Roman domination of Athens, however, indicates a marked shift in the building program from a political to an educational emphasis. Wealthy Roman patrons provided endowments for buildings which encouraged cultivation in the arts and complemented the educational emphasis of sophistic rhetoric. One of the earliest influences of Roman patronage in Athens is seen in the Agrippeion or Odeion of Agrippa. In c. 15 B.C. Marcus Vipsanius Agrippa, the son-in-law of the Emperor Augustus, established an odeion or lecture-concert hall in the Agora (Pausanias 1. 8. 6; Thompson 1950: 31 *passim*). Such structures were frequently used as sites for public orations and instruction (McDonald 1943: 55, 67). Pausanias often used the term "odeion" to refer to the Roman-style theatres and called particular attention to this structure in his work (Pausanias 1. 8. 6). It was Philostratus, however, who confirmed the use of such buildings as places where sophists might give rhetorical displays (*Vitae Sophistarum* 571, 579). The Odeion of Agrippa fell under the patronage of the emperors and was rebuilt into a smaller lecture hall, possibly during the reign of Antoninus Pius in c. 150 (Thompson 1950: 132, 141; Walden 1970: 266–69). Although severely damaged by the Herulian sack of 267, it was replaced by a gymnasium in c. 400 and served as the principal seat of the university until it closed in 529.

Aided by the endowments of Roman patrons, sophists were able to use public buildings and areas of instruction and gain both power and popularity. Under Roman law, Athens was compelled to provide the opportunity for sophists to practice and students to participate (Eunapius, *Vitae Sophistarum* 487). The need to attract students encouraged sophists to display their intellectual abilities in odeions or private lecture theatres and halls of instruction (Eunapius, *Vitae Sophistarum* 483, 487, 489, 492; Walden 1970: 218–23). On occasion, scribes who were experts in rapid dictation would be placed in the center of these theatres to record the speeches of the sophists (Eunapius, *Vitae Sophistarum* 489). Consequently, some of the foremost educators also became highly skilled platform entertainers and used these educational "theatres" as arenas in which to display their rhetorical prowess. Such a

Model of the Odeion, Phase I, seen from the NW, late 1st century B.C.

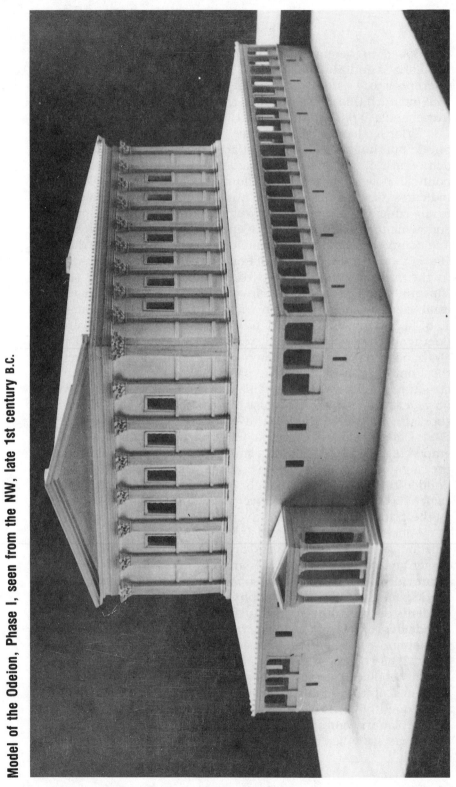

North facade of the Odeion, mid-2nd century A.D., with addition of giants and titans.

Permission granted by the American School of Classical Studies at Athens: Agora Excavations.

practice created an atmosphere where lecture halls became performance theatres and the quality of lectures was frequently measured by bursts of applause and roars of approval (Eunapius, *Vitae Sophistarum* 483–85, 489, 490). Eventually, Athenian odeions became so popular that the emperor Hadrian established the Athenaeum in Rome, a theatre of oratorical display for Greek and Roman sophists and poets, a structure which became the center for the University of Rome (Walden 85).

The construction of odeions and lecture theatres in Athens was not limited to members of the imperial family, but included influential Roman officials as well. Herodes Atticus (c. 107–177), who established himself as both a preeminent sophist and Roman senator, also generously contributed his vast wealth to the Athenian Second Sophistic (Philostratus, *Vitae Sophistarum* 546–51). As a familiar to Hadrian, Antoninus and Aurelius, the Athenian-born sophist Herodes Atticus shared their concern for supporting the cultural heritage of his city. At the death of his wife Regilla in 160, Herodes Atticus established an odeion with a seating capacity of approximately six thousand. It is fitting that this famous sophist would demonstrate his beneficence by constructing one of the final great public buildings in Athens.

Several other buildings, which were constructed or reconstructed during the Athenian Second Sophistic, also indicate strong Roman support for an educational atmosphere. The stoa, a general-purpose building, which frequently served as a site for instruction, as the name of one philosophy and several Socratic dialogues indicate, also came to the attention of the emperors and Roman aristocracy. It was discovered that the Stoa of Attalos and its Bema, which was constructed in the second century B.C., was rededicated to the Emperor Tiberius. Original construction of stoas by Roman patrons was not unheard of; the Stoa of Hadrian is one example. It served as a forecourt to his library.

Although Aulus Gellius argues that Athens actually developed a public library system under the tyrant Pisistratus (d. 527 B.C.), it is commonly believed that Athens did not have a public library until the second century B.C.—and then only through the munificence of Ptolemy (*Noctes Atticae* 1. 272–73 [7. 17]). It comes as no surprise, however, that wealthy Romans considered libraries to be fashionable and actively supported their construction (Plutarch, *Vitae Parallelae: Lucullus* 2. 549–51 [42]; Seneca (the Younger) 9; Merritt, 1947: 170–72). Consistent with their architectural principle of axial symmetry, Romans typically built libraries in pairs, one for Greek work and the other for Latin (MacKendrick 1960: 225–26). The cultural movement of the Second Sophistic in

Athens necessitated a public repository for books, and to this purpose two libraries are known to have been dedicated by or for Romans. The first was the great Library of Titus Flavius Pantainos. Based upon an extant inscription, the construction of this building can be dated to the reign of Trajan, who shared dedication honors with Athena Polias (Merritt 1966: no. 32; Shear 1935: 330–34; Shear 1936: 41–42 [I 2729] and suppl. 8, 268–72).

The second major library to serve the Athenian Second Sophistic was constructed under the auspices of Hadrian (Pausanias 1. 18. 9). The Library of Hadrian, situated close to the Agora, provided a gymnasium and stoa for instruction, as well as space for possible workrooms and repositories for archives. Under Hadrian's generous sponsorship, the rhetorical tradition of the Athenian Second Sophistic attained its pinnacle; Pausanias claimed that Athens prospered most under Hadrian's reign as emperor (Pausanias 1. 20. 7; *Scriptores Historiae Augustae: De Vita Hadriani* 1. 19). The clearest testimony to this sponsorship is inscribed in the Arch of Hadrian. This structure was erected in Athens to mark the boundary of the ancient city and Hadrian's "new" city, which was called Novae Athenae or Hadrianopolis. To the present day, the inscriptions on the sides of the facades can be read (*Inscriptiones Graecae* 3. 401; *Scriptores Historiae Augustae* 1. 62, n. 2):

> This is Athens, Theseus's ancient city.
>
> This is Hadrian's, and not Theseus's city.

The Decline and Fall of Roman Patronage

Imperial patronage continued only through the prosperity of the Roman Empire. The lack of manpower, poor agricultural production, an inability to maintain overextended frontiers and a weakened central government eventually brought an end to the prosperity that supported the Athenian Second Sophistic. Barbarian invasions on Athens began with the Herulian sack of 267. Attempts to check the destruction of the Heruli meant the creation of the Valerian Wall, a Roman fortification built with the stones that came from many of the buildings which the Romans had constructed. Thus, whether by attack or defense, many of the cultural centers in Athens were decimated. The old outer walls were reconstructed in the fifth century, and part of the Agora was occupied by a large gymnasium that is commonly identified with the University.

Like Athens, Rome was unable to withstand barbarian

Regulations of the Library of Pantainos

Permission granted by the American School of Classical Studies at Athens: Agora Excavations.

invasions in the West and fell in 476. This collapse terminated the sponsorship and exposure between two major cities which had lasted for centuries. Isolation between East and West solidified when the Byzantine Empire emerged and Constantinople replaced Rome as the patron of Hellenic literature. Byzantine support of rhetoric is evident in such acts as the *Codex Theodosianus*, a constitution enacted by Theodosius II in 425 which allowed for the sponsorship of both Greek and Roman rhetors and grammarians at Constantinople (Marrou 1956: 307–8; Walden 1970: 147–51).

Byzantine culture was influenced by Hellenic and Hellenistic theories of rhetoric. In general, the influence of Christianity in the East did not severely restrict the study of pagan literature as it did in the Latin West. Unlike the West, there was little conflict between the Church and "pagan" rhetoric, as exemplified by the alliance of Greek and Christian thought in Justinian and Clement. The major restriction, however, was that pagan literature be taught by Christian teachers, as was the case in such great academic centers as Alexandria, Antioch and Gaza. Early Church Fathers were even content that Christians ought to read some pagan texts during their education (Reynolds and Wilson 1968: 41). Several non-Christian Athenian sophists, however, were willing neither to comply with nor conform to Christian doctrines and left.

The unwillingness of Athenian sophists to comply with the notion of a "Christian" education curtailed patronage from Constantinople and prompted Athenian educators to teach at other academic centers. Influential Moslem leaders, for example, welcomed pagan scholars who were banished from Athens (Nicholson 358). Severed from Rome's imperial patronage and unwilling to comply with the Christian principles of the Byzantine Empire, Athens was relegated to the status of a second-class educational center for rhetoric. By the sixth century, the dominance of Christianity suppressed the last of the Second Sophistic in Athens when Byzantine Emperor Justinian closed the pagan university with an edict in 529. The decline of the Roman Empire buried not only the physical remains of the Agora, but the Athenian Second Sophistic as well. After the closing of the university, the Agora was abandoned until the tenth century and covered by the resulting rubble of an uninterrupted occupation of dwellings throughout the Byzantine, Frankish and Turkish periods.

Conclusion

Literary and historical evidence strongly supports the argument that sophists were sponsored and even granted special immunities by influential Romans. Archaeological and epigraphical evidence clearly reveals that the public building programs in Athens shifted from a political emphasis to an academic emphasis, as did rhetoric. During the Athenian Second Sophistic, public building programs were conducted predominantly under the auspices of Roman imperial patronage. The waning power of the Roman Empire and the emergence of the Byzantine Empire resulted in the isolation of Athens from the West. The advent of Christianity and the destruction by barbarians brought the decline of the Athenian Second Sophistic.

The evidence indicates that imperial patronage had a critical effect upon the educational climate of the Second Sophistic in Athens. The parallel rise and decline of the Athenian Second Sophistic with the Roman Empire was not fortuitous. Contrary to the notion that the rhetorical tradition of the Athenian Second Sophistic was more or less autonomous from the Latin West, endowments for individual sophists and cultural building programs by Roman patrons reveal that the flourishing of rhetorical studies during the Athenian Second Sophistic was a direct effect of Roman sponsorship. Unable to sustain itself when support was removed, the Athenian Second Sophistic degenerated to a local function until its eventual termination.

The buildings discussed were centers for the teaching and performance of rhetoric. Yet, if we expand our notion of rhetoric beyond the limitations of the written or spoken word, we may also consider the architecture itself as an act of rhetoric. The cultural buildings sponsored by Romans not only in Athens but throughout the Empire are stable, enduring and symbolic. They are, in their own right, messages about the importance and preservation of these social activities. This point is similar to the argument made by Donovan J. Ochs in *Consolatory Rhetoric: Grief, Symbol, and Ritual in the Greco-Roman Era* (1993). Ochs examines the funerary practices of Greece and Rome; his intent is to explain the rhetorical dimensions of these rituals in two important cultures. "By examining consolatory rituals in the Greco-Roman Era in terms of symbolic behaviors addressed to relevant audiences," Ochs writes, "one can gain new understanding and insight about the human uses of symbols and symbolic behaviors in consolatory settings" (13). To appreciate Ochs' contributions in explicating how rhetoric operates in these sorts of communal activities, we need to extend our appreciation of what is rhetorical *in* such activities and what is rhetorical *about* them. Clearly funerals often prompted occasions for epideictic orations, and understanding the practices of these rituals helps us to understand the genre and the rhetoric itself. Yet, as Ochs argues, the rituals themselves, both in the practices and artifacts, are also symbolic "statements" eliciting messages to participants.

Ochs' point is clear and has implications for our view of the Roman cultural buildings of the Second Sophistic. Romans supported Greek rhetoric in a number of ways. Individuals were encouraged and rewarded because of and for their expertise in rhetoric. Romans helped to insure the continuation of Greek rhetoric by complementing municipal chairs of rhetoric with imperially endowed chairs. Lastly, and relevant to Ochs' parallel findings, the Roman endowment for cultural building programs not only provided the environments for rhetoric but were themselves presentational, rhetorical symbols of their commitment to Greek language arts and education. These other-than-verbal registers (118), as Ochs has shown, should also be included with the oral and written manifestations of rhetoric if we are to grasp not only the environment within which rhetoric was produced but how the physical context is an inextricable part of the rhetoric.

chapter VI

A Study of the Roman Patronage of Greek Oratorical and Literary Contests
The Amphiareion of Oropos

We have seen that Romans supported rhetoric in Athens through patronage of sophists and cultural building programs. Romans supported Greek rhetoric in yet other ways, such as the sponsorship of literary and rhetorical contests at sites throughout Greece. So extensive was Roman support of these events that a recording of this sponsorship would appear like the catalogue of ships in Homer: historically invaluable but tediously long. Archaeological and epigraphical evidence at one sanctuary, the Amphiareion of Oropos, is an excellent illustration of the particular nature and emphasis of Roman support of Greek rhetoric.

Although the Amphiareion of Oropos is virtually unmentioned by ancient authors, epigraphical evidence reveals that for centuries this sanctuary was a frequent site of rhetorical and literary contests as well as a repository of written communication about these events. Based upon fieldwork in Greece and archaeological reports, inscriptions were examined with other archaeological evidence to reconstruct the nature and duration of these events. Even a relatively small site can yield findings of major importance for the history of rhetoric. One of the more important findings of this work is the extensive and enduring support that Rome gave to the study of rhetoric and poetics throughout the Greek-speaking world and how, as a result, the study and practice of Greek rhetoric was made possible by Roman patronage.

In a real sense, as illustrated in the preceding chapter, the study of Hellenic rhetoric is confined to one great city—Athens. Such a perspective is understandable, for written communication providing information about the ancient Greek world often originated from, or was written about, this great political and intellectual center. Most of our knowledge of Hellenic civilization comes from literary evidence transmitted by scribes and refined by scholars over the centuries. In contrast, much of what we know of antiquity from archaeological evidence has been discovered and systematically studied only for a century—a relatively brief amount of time to fully appreciate the Greek world and its relationship to Rome beyond the obvious remains of prominent centers such as Athens. As a preeminent intellectual center, Athens attracted great scholars who, in turn, recorded in detail the events of this city. Other prominent centers, not enjoying the attention Athens received, did not benefit from enduring records.

Thucydides, the foremost historian of classical Athens, was sensitive to the problem that over-attention to Athens could distort the accomplishments of other cities. Thucydides cautioned that centuries after the Peloponnesian War—long after Sparta's modest earthen dwellings crumbled while Athens' magnificent marble structures endured—no one would believe that Sparta had been a force that rivaled Athens (1. 10. 2). Thucydides' caution concerning political history is a lesson that applies as well to the history of rhetoric. Even a cursory reading of George Kennedy's research (1963: 3, 26, 27 ff.; 1975: 280) reveals that rhetoric was taught and practiced actively throughout the Greek-speaking world. Yet, many of these centers for rhetoric did not enjoy the attraction of contemporary writers and, as a result, the literary evidence was not transmitted and their accomplishments faded from recollection as generations passed. These conditions reveal the incompatibility that confronts researchers of the history of rhetoric: an awareness of rhetoric throughout the ancient world but the dependence on "Athenian-oriented" sources for evidence of that history. The resolution to this problem begins by recognizing that standard literary sources need not monopolize evidence and that other types of written communication exist that can both complement traditional philological sources and help resolve the problem of viewing Hellenic rhetoric through Athenian eyes.

Epigraphical sources—written communication inscribed on durable material—were recorded contemporaneously with the event and normally remain unaltered since the original composition.

Unlike traditional literary evidence, epigraphical evidence is not subject to editing and human errors of generations of scribes and scholars; it speaks directly from antiquity. Many such inscriptions, unearthed only during this century, are now available for research and study. A preliminary fieldwork report (Enos 1979) listed twenty-three sites throughout Greece where epigraphical evidence relevant to the history of rhetoric had been recorded and preserved for study. Months of study throughout the country and in the Epigraphical Museum at Athens revealed much larger, more diversified evidence than that collection initially recorded. Continued encouragement from the Greek Ministry of Science and Culture and the American School of Classical Studies at Athens promises the opportunity to study such evidence systematically in the hope of providing new knowledge about ancient rhetoric in Greece.

Part of the current problem in researching the history of Greek rhetoric and its relationship to the Roman revolution is that notions of research persist unchanged in our discipline. It was not uncommon, for example, for Homeric scholars of the last century to limit themselves to texts of the *Iliad* and the *Odyssey* in order to determine whether there actually was a Homer or if Troy ever existed. Heinrich Schliemann, the father of modern archaeology, believed that such debates were best resolved by "the test of the spade." He excavated various sites in Turkey and Greece in order to broaden our view of Homer and the Bronze Age beyond the scope of classical texts. Many of Schliemann's contemporaries strongly criticized such an approach to scholarship, frequently advancing disparaging remarks about how scholars need not grovel in the dirt in order to do research (Ceram 1972: 55–62; Brackman 1974: 159–74; see also, Deuel 1977: 6–7, 13–15, 219–20). Schliemann's innovative, if not sophisticated, methods of research have rewritten much of our knowledge of the Homeric world. Unfortunately, many researchers in classical rhetoric resist efforts such as Schliemann's and perpetuate the armchair, traditional methods of analyzing written communication.

As a means of illustrating the value of such evidence, this chapter reconstructs the history of rhetoric at a sanctuary dedicated to the hero Amphiaraus located near Oropos. Although this site received limited attention from ancient authors (e.g., Pausanias 34. 1–5. Strabo 1. 4. 7; 9. 1. 22; 9. 2. 6. Thucydides 7. 28. 1), it was a repository of written communication that provides valuable information about the history of rhetoric. The written evidence available at this one location should establish the point that the potential for significant findings at numerous sites and museums warrants the attention (and effort) of researchers.

For centuries, the remains of the Amphiareion were buried among plane trees, pines and laurels in the rustic valley where the sanctuary is located. In 1884, the Greek Archaeological Society began systematic excavations under the supervision of Basil Leonardos, which continued without interruption until his death in 1929 (Petracos 1974: 29); later research at the Amphiareion was done under Basil Petracos. The recordings of unearthed inscriptions over the last one hundred years, in addition to on-site examination of source material, reveal that the sanctuary at Oropos regularly held contests in honor of Amphiaraus from at least the fifth century B.C. to the first century A.D. (Petracos 1974: 13, 36)—that is, throughout the five hundred years in which rhetoric was "invented" to its stabilization as a formal discipline. These inscriptions reveal that rhetorical and literary contests held a prominent place in the games and festivals at the Amphiareion for centuries; they provide invaluable evidence of written communication from sources that have been all but totally ignored by historians of rhetoric. This chapter synthesizes epigraphical evidence to determine how the Amphiareion of Oropos became a site for rhetorical display, how such rhetorical activities were sustained for centuries, and the nature of rhetorical displays as revealed by the extant written communication.

The Amphiareion of Oropos:
Pre-Roman Events and Roman Patronage

Oropos is in the coastal district on the northeast frontier between Boeotia and Attica and approximately thirty-one miles from Athens; the city of Oropos is located on the mainland side of the Euripos between Rhamnous and Delion with Eretria on the opposite side. This location, normally favored by pleasant weather during the warm months, was easily accessible by ship and was an active commercial center. Pausanias (34. 1, 2) indicates that twelve stades (approximately 1 1/2 miles) away from Oropos stood the Amphiareion, a site commemorating the divine Amphiaraus, a distinguished warrior and seer from Argos who fought, according to Aeschylus (568–9), as one of the seven against Thebes. A legendary hero from the underworld, Amphiaraus became popular for his abilities as a soothsayer, diviner, and especially a healer (Aeschylus 568–9; Apollodorus 3. 6. 2–4; Pausanias 34.1–5). A cult honoring Amphiaraus was adopted by the Oropians in about the fifth century B.C. and established at a spring that became famous for its healing properties. The therapeutic value of this excellent water and the pleasant surroundings soon made the Amphiareion a popular rehabilitation center for Greeks and later for Romans (Strabo 9. 1. 22; 9. 2. 10–11; Pausanias 34. 3, 4). Various inscriptions, accounts, votive reliefs and even statuary at the Amphiareion, the National Museum at Athens, and the British Museum present and describe the activities of this sanctuary in vivid detail (Petracos 1974: 18–25; *AE*, 43, 9–10 [no. 127] Hyperides 3, 16 ff.).

As is the case with most sanctuaries, the Amphiareion became an active civic center and several extant inscriptions reveal that important documents were preserved there, including treaties, duties pertaining to the temple, catalogues honoring individuals and (central to this study) public records of rhetorical and literary contests (*AE* 43, 9–10 [no. 127], 11–16 [no. 129], 17 [no. 131], 24–25 [no. 139], 43–44 [no. 155]). Specifically, games and festivals were held regularly to honor Amphiaraus, and it is within the written communication of these events that the history of rhetoric at the Amphiareion was recorded.

Epigraphical evidence dated to the time of the Roman Republic reveals that the *agonothetos* had the responsibility of organizing the games (*IG*, nos.416,419,420; *AE*, 43, 33, [no. 148]). According to legend, Amphiaraus was an athletic champion at the Nemean games, and lists of victors at the Amphiareion from the fourth to the first centuries B.C. emphasize athletic contests for men, *epheboi* (young men), and boys in such events as running, wrestling, boxing, the pancrateion, the pentathlon and hoplite racing (*IG*, nos. 414, 415, 416, 418, 419, 420; Apollodorus 3. 6. 4). The Amphiareion of Oropos was not an intellectual center such as Athens but rather a center for display and performance; in fact, the remains of its small theatre are preserved at the site.

Extant evidence indicates that the games were first held at the Amphiareion in about the fifth century B.C., but the earliest epigraphical sources refer to such games in the mid-fourth century B.C. (Petracos 1974: 36; *IG*, no. 414). The period from 387 to 338 B.C. was a time of systemization. The earliest preserved list of victors dates to approximately 366 B.C. (*IG*, no. 414), between the time of Theban occupation and the return of Athenian control. The list reveals that major games were regularly held. Contestants participated in thirty-two known events for men and youth. Among them were: the kitheria, flute, sophistic exercises, the long run, the short run, the double run, the pentathlon, equestrian exercises, wrestling, the pancration, boxing, heavy-armed exercises, a special charioteer event and a chariot drawn by a pair of horses. Victors in these contests came from fourteen locations throughout Greece, but the overwhelming number of victors (sixteen of the thirty-two events) were from Athens. This early inscription clearly indicates that athletic events dominated the contests. "Sophistic Exercises," won by an Athenian named "Pausimaxos," was the sole rhetorical event and appeared with other "artistic" contests. In this respect, the Amphiareion Games were akin to the larger, more prestigious games of Olympia, Delphi and Isthmia. The "Little Amphiareion" was held annually, and the "Great Amphiareion" was held every fourth year. Both offered events that included rhetorical and literary contests (Petracos 1974: 9, 10, 36).

After the Battle of Chaeronea (338 B.C.), Philip II gave the Amphiareion to the Athenians; this administrative change reorganized the festivals and games, expanding the contests beyond athletic events to include more rhetorical performances (Pausanias 34. 1). If the customary multipurpose use of theatres around Greece was followed at the Amphiareion, the sanctuary's theatre would have been the location not only for dramatic events but poetic, rhetorical and musical contests (*IG*, no. 412, lines 26–28). The diversity of rhetorical events is evident in the inscriptions, and it is likely that the small 300-seat theatre was the site for such recorded contests as sophistic declamations, logical and epic encomia (horatory speeches of praise and blame), and the recitation of rhapsodic verse (*IG*, nos. 414, 415/417, 418, 420). Along with the athletic contests mentioned above, these rhetorical contests doubtlessly became standard events; in fact, the list of the first events under the new name of the "Amphiareion and Roman" games is extant and shows that contests for rhapsodes and epic encomia were standard aspects of these performance festivals (Petracos 1974: 40). A number of inscriptions are available and reveal the expansion and diversity of the Amphiareion games (e.g., *IG*, nos. 414, 415, 416, 417, 418, 419, 420). In fact, and as Petracos (1974: 12) indicates, the period from 287 to 146 B.C. was one of great activity for the Amphiareion games. The relevant inscriptions reveal that individuals came from throughout the Greek world for contests in the oral performance of literature, scholarly declamations, dramatic performances and reading, as well as athletic contests.

Although athletic contests are evident throughout the inscriptions, the epigraphical sources describing the Amphiareion games also reveal an active and long-standing interest in rhetorical contests. The myth of Amphiaraus had frequently captured the interests of men of letters and was a source of inspiration for several ancient writers and poets. Even an "interpreter" at the Amphiareion named Iophon the Knossian gave responses in hexameter verse (Pausanias 34. 4). One inscription, probably recorded between 195 and 146 B.C., is actually a joining of two known fragments (*IG*, nos. 415/417), now housed at the Athens Epigraphical Museum (EM 11969). As is true with the list of victors, this inscription indicates that athletic contests dominated the Amphiareion games. Yet, the inscription also indicates that rhetorical events increased and included contestants who were victorious in a variety of events. Many of these rhetorical contests included quite specialized skills: the composed encomium, rhapsodic exercises, poetic comedy, rhetorical exercises in the delivery of (usually) dramatic literature by an interpreter-actor or *hypokrites* (see also: *AE*, 43, 24–25 [no. 139]; Aristotle, *Rhetoric* 1403B, 1404A), and a declamation on the "glad tidings of Roman conquests." Clearly this written communication of events indicates a diversity and sophistication of rhetorical contests not apparent in the earlier inscription. By their position in the inscription, rhetorical events are grouped with literary readings, interpretations of dramatic compositions, as well as a contest to permit epideictic praise to Rome. This latter contest was won by a citizen of Oropos.

The evidence of rhapsodic contests in this late inscription is particularly important, for it provides further evidence of the perpetuation of contests for the presentation of oral literature, a tradition rooted in Homeric literature and a well-established practice during the Classical Period (Plato, *Ion* 530B, *Leges* 658B). In addition, one photographed inscription still under study concerns the rhapsodes at the Amphiareion and may fix the duration of their contests well beyond this date. Recorded epigraphical sources at sites other than the Amphiareion (Enos 1979: 142) indicate that rhapsodic contests and training in the preservation, composition and rendering of oral literature may have continued well into the third century A.D., clearly itself an index of the sustained support of Romans.

As indicated earlier, Romans traditionally were patrons of rhetorical events, and their sponsorship is evident not only in major intellectual centers such as Athens but, as revealed in the inscriptions of the Amphiareion, at sites of rhetorical performance as well. Inscriptions that record victors during the period of Roman domination show an increasing diversity of rhetorical and literary events. One inscription (*IG*, no. 416) dated to the period of the late Roman Republic includes exercises for heralds; these orators often carried a staff or wand as did Homeric bards. They were considered to be messengers of Zeus, providing them with a sort of inviolable status that placed them above desecration. The events for encomia were expanded to include logical encomia, a sort of "honor roll" encomium, and an epic encomium (*IG*, nos. 416, 420, 418). Poetry readings were expanded also and included both readings in heroic verse, satire, rhapsodic declamation, and even new compositions in tragic and comic poetry. Victors in theatrical contests in both old tragedy and comedy were recorded along with the elocution of dramatic literature by a *hypokrites*.

One reason for the continued popularity, and even the endurance, of these rhetorical contests was Roman patronage. The preceding chapter established that Roman patronage was a major force in sustaining the teaching and practice of rhetoric in Athens. It is certainly reasonable to believe that the Amphiareion, under Athenian direction, would also benefit from Roman patronage. An inscription dating back to 156 B.C. shows the Amphiareion games under Roman auspices. From at least 146 B.C., the games flourished under the direct support of Roman sponsorship, particularly (as a victors' list reveals) during the first century B.C. (*AE*, 3, 98–101 [no. 2]; *IG*, nos. 411, 413, 416, 419, 420; *AE*, 43, 37–38 [no. 151]). Following the donation of the Roman dictator Sulla, for example, the Amphiareion games became increasingly elaborate. One inscription (*IG*, nos. 413, 264) records the renaming of the "Amphiareion and Roman" games. The evidence of this Roman participation is available today, for at the site where the stoa was constructed is a series of inscribed statue bases. The first inscription from the East, in a "T" shape, records the list of victors at the "Amphiareion and Roman" games in the first century B.C. (Petracos 1974: 41). Roman patronage of the games is further revealed by an inscription on display at the Amphiareion that records a Roman decree stipulating that taxes collected from the region of Oropos, and its ports Skala and Delphinion, be ceded to the Amphiareion and that such taxes be used to sponsor the games and sacrifices to Amphiaraus (*IG*, no. 413). This decree, currently on display at the site museum (#8), is endorsed by no less a rhetor than Marcus Tullius Cicero (*IG*, no. 413, lines 12, 13). Such epigraphical evidence clearly reveals that sustained support for these rhetorical and literary contests by influential Romans helped to underwrite the events up to the reign of Augustus in the first century A.D.

As we have seen, Roman sponsorship of chairs of rhetoric and cultural building—such as theatres, odeions, and libraries—is well documented from the Republic through the reign of Hadrian, revealing sustained support for rhetoric and literary studies throughout the Empire. In benefiting the arts, Roman support had a direct and pervasive effect on not only the major cities throughout the Empire but even such sanctuaries as the Amphiareion. With the decline of the Roman Empire and the rise of Christianity, sponsorship disappeared and the Amphiareion (similar to other centers) fell into disuse and neglect and eventually was abandoned. For centuries thereafter the ruins of the Amphiareion lay buried— and with them the written communication that would provide primary evidence about the practice of rhetoric in the Greek world as well as the Roman support that made it possible.

Conclusion

The list of inscriptions mentioned above indicates a clear tendency for rhetorical, poetic and theatrical contests to expand to such an extent that they assumed increasing emphasis when compared with athletic contests (*IG*, no. 420). Such an emphasis is in marked contrast to early inscriptions in the fourth century B.C., which had few artistic contests and only a single, broadly termed rhetorical event called "Sophistic Exercises"—an event that never appears in the later inscriptions of the "Amphiareion and Roman" period (*IG*, no. 414). The parallel that existed between the active athletic contests and the viable military power of Greece has been well established since the writings of Homer. What is evident in the inscriptions of the Amphiareion, however, is the diachronic transition from an athletic/military emphasis to an artistic/cultural emphasis in the games. For much of its history, rhetoric has been viewed as preparatory training. When rhetoric was a source of political power during the Classical Period of Athens and the Roman Republic, rhetorical practice reflected training in deliberative and forensic skills that would have a direct, social impact. Poetic composition, with its origins as artistic works, sought to do homage to gods and heroes. During the Roman Empire, the shift in power from a participatory to a centralized political structure de-emphasized the social and political advantages of rhetoric. Similarly, poetic displays evolved to be creations not so much to honor others but the artists who composed them. During the Roman Imperial Period, rhetoric and poetry had already been long-established as synonymous with higher education and cultural refinement. Athletic and military contests had originally been performed at funeral games to honor those slain in battle and as pragmatic exercises for war; best efforts were initially offered to honor gods and fallen heroes (Ochs 1993). These contests eventually honored athletes for little beyond the intrinsic merits of their performance and the honor they brought to their cities. Similarly, rhetorical and literary contests shifted from their pragmatic and religious origins to performance for their own artistic and cultural merits.

The inscriptions at the Amphiareion reflect the transition of power in the Greek world from military to cultural and mirror the findings of those historians of rhetoric who posit that rhetoric survived because it was able to shift emphasis from a political to an educational/cultural source of power during this period of Roman domination. Such an observation is consistent with the preceding chapter dealing with Roman sponsorship of rhetoric in Athens. Particularly during the Athenian domination of the Amphiareion under Roman auspices, this phenomenon is evident in the written communication of the sanctuary.

This chapter provides a number of observations on the art of rhetoric at the Amphiareion and, in turn, a paradigm for continued research. The earliest inscriptions reveal that rhetoric had a place, although limited, in the sacred games of the Amphiareion. These rhetorical events expanded in number and specialization over the centuries. Rhetorical events were consistently listed early in the list of victors and in the same category with poetic, musical, theatrical and literary contests. Participants came from throughout the Greek world. Roman patronage and support appears to have encouraged an interest in these forms of declamatory and epideictic rhetoric, for the latest inscriptions emphasize rhetorical displays as popular artistic events and not preparatory exercises for politics. The composition of these rhetorical events indicates that such displays were seen as literary entertainment and were far removed from the political and forensic rhetoric that was such a dominant social force in fifth-century B.C. Athens.

The nature of such rhetorical displays at the Amphiareion would be unknown to modern historians of rhetoric were it not for the epigraphical evidence. Whether the Amphiareion is a microcosm of the sort of rhetoric practiced in similar sanctuaries, or in Greece herself, can only be verified through similar field studies, particularly in the remote areas of Greece. The findings discussed here offer evidence to help provide a better understanding of the history of rhetoric, but new sources await continued study (e.g., *SEG*, no. 427). Given the relative size of the site at the Amphiareion, continued fieldwork at large sites, where more detailed and complex holdings are centered, offers great possibilities. Investigation of the written communication found at such sites will yield evidence about the contributions of rhetoric irretrievable by other methods.

chapter VII

Epilogue
Rhetoric in the Greek-Speaking East and the Latin-Speaking West

We have seen that one of the many impressive qualities of rhetoric has been its endurance. Grounded by precepts of expediency and contingency, rhetoric has transcended both cultures and time. In spite of strong and persistent opposition, rhetoric has struggled and survived as an academic discipline, but not without great effort. At no time was the struggle for survival greater than at the fall of the Roman Empire and the rise of Christianity in the Latin West. The fall of the Roman Empire not only severed the Greek-East from the Latin-West, it severely restrained the dynamic and interactive relationship between Greek and Roman rhetoric. Rhetoric in both East and West managed to survive, but the autonomous strains of rhetoric that developed because of this isolation affected their natures for almost a millennium.

Those born in the dawning of the Roman Empire were beneficiaries of a culture that was grounded in rhetorical tradition. Virtually every prominent statesman of the preceding generations had been influenced by rhetoric. Marcus Antonius, Julius Caesar, Gaius Pompeius Magnus, Marcus Tullius Cicero and Quintus Hortensius Hortalus all varied in their political practices and party politics during the Roman Republic. Nonetheless, these men, and many prominent Romans like them, shared one overriding advantage: rhetoric had been a central emphasis in their education.

As we learned earlier, the Roman love for military heroes also made the battlefield an expedient path to the Senate. During the Republic, the ideal Roman leader could amass weapons of eloquence and military prowess which created a positive political image called *dignitas*, thereby meeting the highest standards of Roman culture (Enos and Schnakenberg 1993). When this excellence was achieved, the result was a Julius Caesar or an Augustus. Few Romans, however, could excel in both military and verbal battles. The other routes to political power in the Republic were through tremendous wealth or an aristocratic heritage. Yet several individuals who lacked the appropriate ancestry, vast financial resources or military sagacity could utilize an additional avenue of success in Roman society—the power of rhetoric. Cicero was the most prominent example of someone who attained tremendous success despite lacking the traditional methods of acquiring political power. In essence, rhetoric survived and blossomed in the Republic because it was a primary source of power for political success. In a society where the primary form of communication was oral, rhetoric was imperative.

When Augustus established his Principate in 23 B.C. and transformed the Republic to the Empire, he created an autocracy that virtually eliminated the need for rhetoric as a political tool. Yet, instead of waning, rhetoric flourished within the educational system of the Empire (Duff 1964: 25–33). In the classical educational pattern of Rome, a young child was instructed "in the bosom of one's mother" (*in gremio matris*) until about the age of seven. From the age of seven, children began a course of study in three distinct levels, under the respective guidance of the *litterator*, the *grammaticus* and the *rhetor*. The *litterator*, or *ludi magister*, presented basic courses in reading, writing and arithmetic for both boys and girls from the ages of seven until about eleven years of age. The next level of education came with the twelve-to-fifteen age group and was under the direction of the *grammaticus*. The educational emphasis was general knowledge as a preparation for studies in rhetoric. According to Quintilian (1. 9. 6), the main exercises were in composition, such as the training in moral maxims (*sententiae*), themes of ethical value (*chriae*), outlines of character (*ethologiae*) and brief poetic stories (*narratiunculae*).

After these two levels of education, the student entered the school of the *rhetor*, the height of the educational system. Rhetorical education emphasized the career of the advocate for pupils who entered these schools at about the age of sixteen. The emphasis in legal rhetoric is understandable. Political oratory lost its potency when the Republic shifted to an Empire. Sanctioned avenues of expression, those that operated within the the imperial system, became the emphasis for rhetorical instruction. The legal system—pleading within courtly protocol and epideictic or artistic expression—evolved as the dominant modes of expression. Rhetoric survived throughout the Empire because to exclude it would deny access to the intellectual culture of Rome herself.

As discussed earlier, other emperors recognized and supported the utility of rhetoricians. In spite of the imperial patronage of rhetoric and its popularity the discipline did come under attack. In the eyes of men such as Tacitus (*Dialogus de Oratoribus* 35), rhetoric was a discipline which had lost its relevance and now concerned itself with self-aggrandizement. Yet rhetoric managed to survive throughout the Empire because it was the educational tool of a culture which relied on rhetoricians as models and a source of power in securing state control through imperial patronage. Its preservation was aided because the cultural heritage of the Republic and Empire presented no serious conflict. Rhetoric from the late Empire to the early Middle Ages, however, would receive the greatest threat to its survival with the cultural shift from paganism to Christianity.

The Edict of Milan (313), issued by the Emperor Constantine, marked the recognition of Christianity as a tolerated religion of the Roman Empire. The deathbed conversion of Constantine (337) signaled the emergence of a new institution to challenge the survival of rhetoric. In many respects, rhetoric and Christianity were diametrically opposed. Rhetoric was grounded in probability and skepticism, while early Christianity fostered mysticism and unquestioned faith. Further, rhetorical education primarily aimed at worldly success. Individuals studied rhetoric to attain status and power, often by becoming competent lawyers and administrators. Christianity, however, was not concerned with worldly success but with the methods by which eternal life could be attained. The material possessions and sophistic vanity of imperial rhetoric were in direct contrast to the poverty and humility advocated by the early Christians. In addition, rhetoric operated from an entirely different worldview than Christianity. Rhetoricians lauded heroes such as Aristotle and Cicero as well as the pagan gods of mythology. Further, pagan literature was by no means sacred and quite often open to dispute. Many Christians found it inconsistent to honor any men other than Christ and his followers or any literature except that which they perceived as divinely inspired. It seemed that rhetoric would collapse under the weight of an emerging Christian Empire. Yet rhetoric continued to survive, primarily because influential Christians recognized its adaptability and usefulness as a source of spiritual power.

Although rhetoric and Christianity often came into conflict, there was enough common ground to win the approval of prominent Latin Fathers. As M. L. Clarke (1966) explained: "a Christian leader in the early centuries was a writer and speaker, teacher, controversialist, letter writer, preacher, one who used to the full the written and spoken word" (150). Christians could not avoid the influence of rhetorical tradition. Such Latin fathers as Tertullian, Minutius Felix, Lactantius, Ausonius and Prudentius were all professors of rhetoric. In the East, St. Basil, the son of a rhetorician, and John Chrysostom were both students of pagan rhetoricians. Nevertheless, Christian leaders including Tertullian (*De Anima* 39) denounced the imitation of pagan authors, but as Ferdinand Lot argued, the Roman had the poison of rhetoric in his blood (1931: 164). The freedom of this classical spirit was too great a temptation for St. Jerome and St. Augustine to ignore. Moreover, as Christianity was emerging, the pagan West was experiencing a renaissance of Greek and Latin rhetoricians under the "Second Sophistic," which extended from approximately the second to the fourth Christian centuries (Baldwin 1959: 8, n. 10). Rather than fight neo-sophists such as Philostratus, who promoted non-Christian oratory, some early Church fathers began to use ancient models judiciously and to study the precepts of their pagan counterparts. Yet Church opposition to pagan rhetoric was tremendously strong, and the internal conflict of Church fathers between the intellectual pleasure of pagan literature and the allegiance to Scripture is well illustrated by St. Jerome, who suffered a severe identity crisis from his inability to dislike the reading of Cicero and Plautus (Clarke 1966: 148).

The resistance that Church fathers held toward rhetoric has an earlier parallel with the opposition of patrician leaders of the Roman Republic. As discussed earlier, influential Roman Republicans were initially hesitant to adopt Greek systems of rhetoric. They feared not the adequacy of rhetoric but the opposite—rhetoric's power to persuade. Centuries later, Church fathers also had initial impressions about rhetoric that led them to believe that it was a threat. Church fathers saw rhetoric grounded in worldly concerns and personal glorification. This view of rhetoric created a dilemma since, as with the Republic, the social and educational values of rhetoric could not be denied.

The advantages of rhetoric to early Christians was obvious. In most religious sects, teachings outside the established dogma would have been excluded. The Christian priest, however, was more than the administrator of rituals; he was the shepherd of his flock.

Leaders of the Church had to be educated men if they wished, as Commodian did, to instruct the common man in Christianity. Thus, to be an educated Christian leader in the late Empire and early Middle Ages, one was compelled to continue studying the poets and prose writers of Greece and Rome as well as the Scriptures. Unfortunately, St. Jerome could never fully resolve his Christian humanism, and his only recourse was to remove himself to Bethlehem and escape the temptations of a corrupt world while working on his famous Vulgate Bible. The best resolution St. Jerome's conscience could make toward the conflict is seen in the introduction to his Latin Bible, where the Numbers contain "the mysteries of all arithmetic," the Book of Job has "all the laws of dialectic," and the Psalmist is "our Simonides, Pindar, Alcaeus, Horace, and Catullus" (Curtius 1963: 73). Yet St. Jerome could not fully resolve the cultural challenge of uniting rhetorical education with Christianity. Indeed, the early years of the Middle Ages would have been bleaker had it not been for the genius of St. Augustine, who recognized and promoted the study of rhetoric as a tool for strengthening Christianity. It was St. Augustine who baptized rhetoric into Christianity.

St. Augustine has been called the first writer on Christian preaching and the last of the important rhetorical teachers of the Empire (*Ancient Greek and Roman Rhetoricians* 19–21). St. Augustine, a former professor of rhetoric at Carthage, Rome and Milan, deserves a good deal of credit for helping to unite pagan rhetoric with Christianity, a resolution which some early Church fathers had advocated but were unable to fully accomplish. It was while teaching rhetoric at Milan (*Confessions* 5. 13.) that St. Augustine was drawn to the eloquent St. Ambrose. Through St. Ambrose, St. Augustine realized that he could mold his own rhetorical training and Ciceronian philosophy (*Confessions* 3. 4.) into a Christian rhetoric that could be used to interpret and proclaim the Scriptures.

Greek Church fathers prior to St. Augustine, such as Gregory of Nyssa, exposed the falsity and pedanticism of the Second Sophistic—but could not dismiss its impact. St. Augustine's *De Doctrina Christiana* excluded the paganism of the Second Sophistic, incorporated the precepts of rhetorical doctrine into Christian education and emerged with a new era of Christian rhetoric. St. Augustine converted rhetoric to Christianity; he assimilated principles and topics of rhetoric into a system that was compatible with the Christian objective of winning converts. Modifying, rather than opposing, rhetoric gave Christians a system of expression that rivaled the pagan-oriented Second Sophistic.

Under the auspices of Christian rhetoric, pagan literature could be studied not for its own sake but as indirect models to facilitate the expression of Christian doctrine. In effect, St. Augustine challenged the popularity of the Second Sophistic by promoting not only the study of non-Christian authors but some of the very tenets of the Second Sophistic (Baldwin 52). Sophists taught rhetoric with an eye toward success in the city of man; St. Augustine offered a rhetoric that instructed with a perspective directed toward success in the city of God.

Analyzing *De Doctrina Christiana* reveals St. Augustine's concept of the Christian rhetor. The ideal rhetor in the tradition of St. Augustine would be a staunch defender and professor of truth— that is, Christian doctrine. The goals are Ciceronian: to educate, to delight and to persuade (*Orator* 69). The province, however, is Christian literature, and for this the rhetor ought to have both wisdom and eloquence. Perspicuity is the keynote for effective instructive speaking for St. Augustine, and the perfect rhetor will try to instruct before he persuades. The most important element of Augustinian rhetoric is the morality of the rhetor. The rhetor's goal is not to debate either side of the question equally well but rather to speak only for the just, holy and good. Through the piety of his prayers, the ideal rhetor is a petitioner before he is a speaker. For St. Augustine, Christ is the truth, and the ideal rhetor seeks the truth.

St. Augustine's treatise illustrates how rhetoric not only survived Christianity but became assimilated into it. Rhetoric became a means of instructing and persuading a pagan world to adopt Christianity. The absolutism of a Christian rhetoric became a sword for the defenders of the faith to wield. In essence, rhetoric survived Christianity because its value as an educational tool was too great to be ignored. Yet, even before St. Augustine was resolving the conflict between rhetoric and Christianity, a new power was emerging to threaten the survival of rhetoric and the Empire itself— the barbarian invasions.

Edward Gibbon's famous statement that the Roman Empire was a stupendous fabric was no exaggeration; scores of scholars have proposed dozens of theories explaining why it finally collapsed, severing East and West. The lack of manpower, poor agricultural production, a weakened central government and the inability to maintain over-expanded frontiers which extended from the Rhine to the Danube and Tigris and Euphrates are all factors which help to explain the success of the barbarian invasions and the localization of authority. The change of the Empire in the early Middle Ages, moreover, fostered the growth of three distinct cultures: Byzantium, Islam, and the Frankish kingdoms of the West. The survival of rhetoric in the Greek East and Islam is outside the scope of this work, but a few brief observations about its survival in various forms will help reinforce our appreciation for the interaction which defined rhetoric during the Roman Empire and its subsequent metamorphosis.

The Eastern portion of the Roman Empire centered around Constantinople (formerly Byzantium and now Istanbul) and included parts of Europe and Western Asia. Many prominent Greek cities in the East besides Constantinople continued as important centers in the Roman Empire. Ephesus, located south of Izmir in Turkey, was considered the Roman capital of Asia Minor. The Byzantine culture of the East had never lost the influence of the Hellenic and Hellenistic theories of rhetoric; the Second Sophistic rekindled such preferences in the Greek East. Further, there was less conflict with the Church and rhetoric, as exemplified by the alliance of Greek and Christian thought in Justinian (483–565) and Clement. Beginning with Constantine's acceptance of Christianity, the absolute rule of Byzantine emperors was supported by the Christian Church, which eventually became the Eastern Orthodox Church. As a rule, Byzantine emperors also supported rhetoric— with the stipulation that it be compatible with Christian doctrine. Early Church fathers were content that Christians ought to read some pagan texts during their education (Reynolds and Wilson 1968: 41). The influence of Christianity in the East did not severely restrict the study of pagan literature, as it did in the Latin West. The major restriction was that pagan literature be taught by Christian teachers; this was the case in great Greek academic centers such as Alexandria, Antioch and Gaza. The teaching of pagan philosophy by pagan instructors was not permitted— exemplified by Justinian's closing of the schools of philosophy at Athens. In spite of these restrictions, the Church in the East assimilated classical culture far more readily than the West. Unlike their Western counterparts, rhetoricians in the East had far less need of a champion such as St. Augustine.

By 850 the Byzantine Empire, because of its better centralized bureaucracy, more efficient government and superior finances, could promote the basic educational institutions it had always sustained and encourage an intensification of scholarly activity. Scholarship became so lauded that even the great patriarch Photius himself was a classical scholar. The Imperial government was the chief patron of learning and art and produced such great scholars as Leo VI (the Wise) and Constantine VII. In addition, a large number of handbooks on the study of rhetoric, the Attic orators, and especially Demosthenes were published throughout the East (Reynolds and Wilson 1968: 38). Byzantine scholars compiled manuals on nearly every subject including rhetoric, and great libraries were established to house the collections of classical Greek literature (Sullivan 1963: 97). Since the West forgot how to read Greek after Boethius (c. 480–524), a good amount of the credit for the survival of Greek rhetorical treatises must go to the Byzantine culture; the remainder of the credit goes to Islam.

Prior to 750 the cultural tradition of the Moslem world was little more than a continuation of Greco-Roman, Persian and Indian cultures fostered by large and active communities of Jews, Christians and Zoroastrians. The Moslem Empire began in 750 and continued to 1258. From 750–850 the cultural revival of the early Abbasid period produced translations of much Greek, Persian and Indian learning into Arabic—thereby transmitting treatises to Moslem scholars. The breadth of preserved and translated material was tremendous, covering virtually every known discipline including rhetoric. The chief center for the scholarly translators, who were often Persian and Syrian rather than Arab, was Bagdad. The Abbasid renaissance parallels both the time and purpose of the Carolingian renaissance, which will be treated later. Yet the meritorious efforts of the Carolingian renaissance to preserve Latin works was not as effective as the encyclopedic collections of diverse and rare philosophical Greek works recaptured by the Moslems (Sullivan 1963: 97). Through the efforts of the Moslems, Platonic and Aristotelian works were preserved. Even as late as 1905, fragments of orations by Lysias were discovered at Oxyrhynchus. In essence, rhetoric survived in the East because it was assimilated and utilized by both Byzantine and Moslem cultures and because there was no direct threat to its existence.

In the ancient province of Gaul, strong attempts were made by the cultivated leisure class to preserve the symbols of Romanism in a waning Empire plagued by barbaric invasions. In a sense, Gaul was facing the future by looking backward to the past. Frantically adhering to tradition but steadily converting to Christianity, Gaul was the last territory of the ancient world and the last stronghold of the Roman school. One of the first, and perhaps the greatest of the rhetorical schools of Gaul was at Bordeaux. The early years of the academy produced their most famous *grammaticus* and *rhetor*, Ausonius. Securing goodwill as the tutor of Gratian, Ausonius gained prominent state offices, such as the Praetorian praefecture of Italy (377) and Gaul (378), and eventually the consulship (379). A professed pagan, Ausonius expressed his gratitude to the Emperor with his *Actio Gratiarum*, which Gibbon called "a servile and insipid piece of flattery" and professed that Ausonius's "poetical" fame condemned the taste of a bad age (1845, 2: 539, ns. 1, 2). An expert in meter and diction, Ausonius's claim as the best of a bad age was his ability to turn a stanza on anything. His rhetorical wordplay was rarely beyond classroom *declamatio*. Among the Bordeaux rhetoricians, Ausonius was the leader in the mastery of rhetoric and poetic; as long as the sophistic tradition persisted in the Roman schools of Gaul, Ausonius was the model to be lauded.

The infiltration of the Germanic peoples reached migration proportions by 375 when they were forced into the Empire by the invasion of the Asiatic Huns. The Visigoths, Arian Christians disenchanted about the good faith of Roman officials, defeated Emperor Valen at Adrianople in 378 and were ceded territory within the Empire. Eventually, they attacked Italy and sacked Rome by 410. The barbarian "invasions" of the fifth century were less often actual invasions and more often infiltrations of small groups of barbarians migrating into the Roman Empire and establishing farm lands on the frontier borders or within the Empire itself. Furthermore, as Robert S. Hoyt (1966: 47) indicated, German kings who did invade the western Empire with armies came to conquer and rule, not to destroy. By the fourth and fifth centuries, when the barbarians finally broke into the Empire, Roman influence had penetrated into the North through commercial interaction. Thus, exposure between cultures had been established for some time prior to the collapse of the Empire. Further, the Roman army, overextended and depleted in manpower, had incorporated both individuals and whole tribes of barbarians into the military (Hoyt 1966: 51). In some respects, the "decline and fall" of the Empire is better understood as a process of assimilation and replacement.

A series of other invaders followed the Visigoths. The Vandals migrated through France and Spain into North Africa where they settled in 439 and later sailed to attack Sicily and Rome in 455. The Burgundians occupied southern Gaul, the Angles and Saxons from the North Sea coasts moved into Flanders and England in 449, and the Huns swept into Italy in 452. By 476 the Germanic leader Odoacer deposed Romulus Augustus, the last Emperor, putting an end to the western Empire. Odoacer was killed by the Ostrogoths, who as Arian Christians attempted to preserve Roman institutions and culture. Their king, Theodoric (493–526), became the ruler of Italy.

While Theodoric was securing his empire in Italy, Clovis, a Catholic leader of the Franks, succeeded in defeating a Roman army at Soissons in 486 and became ruler of all Gaul. Like Theodoric, Clovis fused Germanic and Roman ways of living and retained

Roman institutions and culture. Of all the Germanic states, only Clovis's Merovingian dynasty survived and expanded south and east. The Ostrogoths were attacked and eventually defeated in 562 by a Byzantine army sent to reconquer Italy. The Visigoths were expelled from southern Gaul by the Franks in 507, migrated to Spain, and were eventually conquered by the Moslems. The Angles and Saxons were isolated in Britain, where they formed petty warring kingdoms. Thus, the Franks under Clovis emerged as the political foundation of the Empire; under the Merovingian dynasty strong attempts were made to preserve both patristic achievements and those elements of pagan culture which were considered important. The attempt of the early Franks to preserve their Roman legacy is best illustrated by their efforts at transmitting classical literature, particularly rhetorical treatises, in the schools of Gaul.

Few towns in Gaul of any size were without their *grammatici* and *rhetores* in the fourth and fifth centuries. Marseilles, Autun, Lyon, Bordeaux, Toulouse, Narbonne, Poitiers and Treves were typical centers of instruction in Gaul. These academies praised Tertullian, Cyprian, Victorinus of Pattau, Arnobius and Lactantius as prominent writers of the Latin Church, but there were no grammatical or rhetorical treatises suitable as schoolbooks other than the pagan authors. The rhetorical tradition, the educational ideal that rhetoric was the mark of the cultured man, was a quality inherited by the Gallic scholars. The Church created no new educational systems to rival the precepts of rhetoric. Furthermore, rhetoric flourished in Gaul, not only because it continued to be instrumental in education but also, as Theodore J. Haarhoff has argued, because the Gauls possessed a natural aptitude for eloquence (160). In the *Herakles* of Lucian there is a picture of the Gallic Hercules who leads men "by fine chains attached to his tongue and their ears, and they follow gladly though it is in their power to break away" (160, n. 2).

Rhetoric also survived in Gaul because of the heavy emphasis on preaching. The precepts of oratory were utilized because of the tremendous power which rhetoric could exercise over its Gallic Christian listeners. Ennodius, the fifth-century Bishop of Pavia, and Hilary of Poitiers both incorporated affected eloquence into their oratory (Haarhoff 162, 163, 167). Rhetoric, however, was still strongly criticized by many Church fathers who advocated a direct style of preaching, and Sulpicius Severus and Claudius Victor of Marseilles strongly denounced the pagan schools as well as pagan authors. Yet, in spite of her criticisms, the Church recognized that the old system of rhetorical education was not only systematically organized but most importantly was the traditional method of learning. According to Haarhoff, "everything that was not cut according to the traditional pattern . . . tended to be despised, and this was the attitude towards the Christians in the educational world of the day" (170–71). Therefore, the Gallic monks of the Church set out to copy and thereby preserve ancient rhetorical treatises and traditional education. The rhetorical tradition which these schools of Gaul actually did preserve is best seen both in the prominent rhetoricians they produced and the textbooks they used throughout the fifth to seventh centuries.

The most prominent Gallic rhetorician after Ausonius was Sidonius Apollinaris, the fifth-century Bishop of Auvergne (Baldwin 78). Much of what we know about the country life of Gallic noblemen comes from the epistles of the orator Sidonius Apollinaris. The panegyrics, letters and poems of this Christian bishop illustrate his adroitness in *ars dictaminis* (the art of letter writing) and his perpetuation of *declamatio* in the tradition of Ausonius. Educated at Lyon, Sidonius Apollinaris represents the Gallic love of the past, rhetorical education and obsession with style (Baldwin 78). Sidonius Apollinarius, like earlier Gallic teachers, tended to blend rhetoric and poetic, even to the extent of misapplying Horace's poetry as a model for declamation. Also like most prominent Gallic rhetoricians, Sidonius Apollinaris was a figure in the political structure and the familiar of Theodoric, king of the Ostrogoths in Gaul (Gibbon 1845, 3: 217). More importantly, the rhetoric and poetic of fifth-century Gaul are exemplified in Sidonius Apollinaris's faithful preservation of the sophistic tradition of *declamatio*.

Severance and Restraint

The preceding historical account has shown the fracturing of the Roman Empire, the severance of East and West, and the ensuing historical and cultural constraints on the study of Greek and Roman rhetoric. The cumulative effect of the collapse of the Roman Empire and the splintering of its remnants on rhetoric was the emergence of four rhetorical "traditions" which existed up to the Middle Ages. These traditions are carefully detailed by James J. Murphy in his *Rhetoric in the Middle Ages*. The first tradition is the Aristotelian tradition, including the *Rhetoric*, *Topica* and *Sophistici Elenchi*. The emphasis was predominantly philosophical and was virtually non-existent in the Gallic schools but was preserved in the Byzantine and Moslem cultures. The second tradition is the Ciceronian tradition, encompassing Cicero's *De Inventione* and

Rhetorica ad Herennium plus (to some degree) Quintilian's *Institutio Oratoria*. These were the works from which the Latin West derived much, if not all, of their rhetorical training from approximately the third to the ninth century. The third tradition is the Grammatical tradition which, as has been shown, was inseparably linked with rhetoric by such Gallic rhetoricians as Ausonius and Apollinaris. The major treatises in this movement include the *Ars Mainor* of Aelius Donatus and the *Ars Poetice* of Horace. The fourth and final tradition is the Sophistic tradition, which incorporated the classroom exercises of *declamatio* and *progymnasmata*. It flourished primarily from 50–400 during the Second Sophistic but remained in Gallic schools. The chief treatises in the Sophistic tradition were works that stressed declamation. Lucius Annaeus Seneca's *Controversiae et Suasoriae* and Hermogenes' *Progymnasmata* are two such works that were brought directly into the Middle Ages by Priscian's *De Preexercitamentis*.

Earlier we saw how Republican Romans assimilated much of Greek rhetoric into their own theories and how Greeks of that period ignored Roman contributions. We learned how Romans during the Imperial Period sponsored and benefited from Greek rhetoric and sophistic education. Again, little was taken by Greek rhetoricians from Romans beyond patronage. With the fall of the Empire, contact between East and West diminished considerably. At this point, however, the West had fashioned and solidified its canons of rhetoric. Schools of rhetoric in the Greek-speaking East continued to function autonomously from the rhetoric of the West, even to the extent of establishing their own canons of rhetoric. "By the end of the fifth century," writes George Kennedy, " a standard rhetorical corpus had emerged which remained authoritative for Greeks for the next thousand years and which still survives complete" (1980: 185). The Greek canon of rhetoric centered not so much on particular concepts—as did the Latin canons of invention, arrangement, style, memory and delivery—but on prominent works. The *Progymnasmata* of Aphthonius, *On Staseis* by Hermogenes, *On Invention* (which may have been written by Hermogenes), Hermogenes' *On Ideas*, and the unknown author of *On Method* were the core for Byzantine rhetoric (Kennedy 1980: 185). These works, as Kennedy observes, place a strong emphasis on composition and invention, particularly the study of heuristics (186).

The rhetorical tradition preserved by the Gallic schools was predominantly Ciceronian. At least some parts of Quintilian's *Institutio Oratoria* were known to both Ausonius and Sidonius

Apollinaris, and probably most rhetoricians of Gaul (Baldwin 89). Students used Cicero's *De Inventione* and the *Rhetorica ad Herennium*. From these Ciceronian works the Gallic rhetorician Gaius Chirius Fortunatianus (fourth century) composed an abbreviated compendium. It was from such compendia that commentaries relating to rhetoric would be produced in subsequent centuries. Three of the most influential are Martianus Capella's *De Nuptiis de Philologiae et Mercurii*, a fifth-century treatise that is credited with solidifying the *trivium* and *quadrivium*; the *Institutiones Divinarum et Saecularium Litterarum* of the Roman statesman and writer, Cassiodorus (d. 575); and Archbishop Isidore (570–636) of Seville's *Isidori Hispalensis Etymologarium sive Originum*.

Although the schools of Gaul should receive credit for their attempts to preserve rhetorical treatises, their influence was felt mainly by the upper classes. The Frankish Merovingian dynasty of Clovis could not long sustain, let alone foster, their cultural legacy. The ravages of conquest and barbarism were not conducive to the perpetuation of Latin literature in the Roman schools of Gaul. Attempts were made to preserve the works of antiquity by Cassiodorus and Isidore, but the continual destruction of warfare and the Christian hostility to pagan literature gave rhetoric a slim chance of survival. Further, the compendia of rhetoric had produced a series of abridged and diluted handbooks which, over the centuries, supplanted the classical rhetorical treatises in their original form. If this process were allowed to continue, those rhetorical works of Gaul would have preserved little more than the titles, for the contents had become so capsulated and mutated over the centuries that the substance bore only a faint resemblance to the copies of Antiquity. If the rhetorical treatises of Antiquity were to be preserved in full, a renaissance was required which, fortunately, came with the establishment of the Carolingian Empire.

During the waning of the schools of Gaul and prior to the dawn of the Carolingian Empire, the bulk of Latin literature was still extant; among these texts were varied selections of Cicero (Reynolds and Wilson 1968: 71). The machinery for the transmission of rhetoric to later ages was being established in the monastic libraries and scriptoria of the intellectual centers of Gaul. It was through monastic centers such as Vivarium, founded by Cassiodorus sometime after 540, that the pagan authors would find a place in both the library and program (Reynolds and Wilson 1968: 72). The tradition of Vivarium was perpetuated by famous monasteries such as Monte Casino and Bobbio. Yet the preservation of Latin literature, and specifically rhetorical treatises that have survived, could have been accomplished only in the climate of a more sympathetic attitude. This positive attitude was attained by Irish and English scholars of the seventh and eighth centuries, such as Aldhelm (c. 639–709) and the Venerable Bede (673–735). The missionary and educational zeal of the Continental Christians had inadvertently fostered an intellectual rebirth of Anglo-Latin culture which would eventually rebound back to the Continent in the late eighth and ninth centuries and culminate in the cultural revival of the Carolingian renaissance.

In 741 Charles Martel, Mayor of the Palace in the Frankish kingdom, was succeeded by his two sons, Pepin the Short and Carloman. Charles Martel governed the last four years of his life with an empty throne, since the establishment of a puppet king provoked Merovingian noblemen to revolt. When Pepin and Carloman became mayors, the noblemen rebelled, but by 747 Pepin had firmly established his power and already installed Childric III on the throne. After Carloman retired to the monastery of Monte Casino, Pepin appointed himself king, was anointed by the papal representative, St. Boniface, and thus supplanted the Merovingian dynasty with the Carolingian dynasty. Pepin strongly allied the Church with the new Frankish kingdom, and by the "Donation of Pepin" the Pope received the Exarchate of Ravenna. The height of the Carolingian Empire, however, came with Pepin's son, Charlemagne (768–814). Under the rule of Charlemagne the western Empire was reestablished.

As ruler of the Franks, Charlemagne first unified his own noblemen, came to the assistance of the pope by defeating the Lombards in 773–774, and assumed the "iron crown" of the Lombard king. Having incorporated northern Italy into a union with the Frankish kingdom, Charlemagne then spent the next thirty-two years defeating the heathen Saxons (772–804) and placing other German tribes under Carolingian authority. Charlemagne then established the defensive Spanish march south of the Pyrenees (778–801), subordinated the barbarian Slavs in eastern Bavaria, and between 791 and 795 crushed the raiding Asiatic Avars who had settled on the banks of the upper Danube. By 800 Charlemagne controlled an area larger than any king had ruled since the Roman emperors of the fourth century. By his own authority, Charlemagne was both king of the Franks and King of the Lombards, as well as Patricius Romanorum, when he was crowned emperor by Pope Leo III. Even with all this success, the Carolingian Empire that was solidified by Charlemagne would not last longer than the two generations which survived him, but the cultural achievements which he sponsored helped to secure the survival of rhetoric in the West more than in any other era.

The key distinction of the Carolingian renaissance in the revival of rhetorical treatises lies in Charlemagne's influence in the palace schools. Although both Charles Martel and Pepin the Short had maintained schools within the central court, Charlemagne, in the words of Robert S. Hoyt, "transformed the palace school into a serious educational enterprise, and from it there emanated throughout the empire new standards of education and of scholarly interest" (1966: 155). In a very real sense, Charlemagne promoted a one-man renaissance, for through his patronage there was a renewed zeal not only for early patristic achievements but for pagan literature as well. The secular and ecclesiastical administration of Charlemagne's empire required a larger number of learned priests and administrators. Charlemagne could not write, and probably could not read, but he recognized the weakness of an illiterate clergy and therefore brought to his court the most learned scholars of Latin Christendom. The poet Theodulfus from Christian Spain, Paul the Deacon (who wrote the *History of the Lombards*), the Franks Einhard and Angilbert and the Irish scholar Dungal were all intellectuals whom Charlemagne had brought to court. Yet, by far the most influential scholar, and the individual who aided most in perpetuating rhetoric, was Alcuin of York.

In general terms, one of Alcuin's prominent achievements was his promotion, under the auspices of Charlemagne, of Caroline minuscule, an extremely legible style of handwriting which used both small and capital letters. Replacing the Merovingian cursive scrawl and other elaborate styles of writing, Alcuin used the Caroline minuscule as the medium by which to transmit the surviving works of antiquity. The purpose of collecting and copying these classical manuscripts was to increase the number of books for the education of the clergy and administrators. There is an estimation that 90 percent of the Latin literary works of antiquity have been transmitted by their duplication in Carolingian scriptoria and preserved in Carolingian cathedral and monastery libraries (Hoyt 1966: 156). Out of this great corpus of Latin literature several rhetorical treatises were preserved: Cicero's orations, including the *In Verrem*, *In Catilinam*, *Pro Rege Deiotaro*, *Orationes Philippicae*, *Pro Fonteio* and *In Pisonem*; rhetorical treatises, including the *Rhetorica ad Herennium*, and Cicero's *De Inventione* and *De Oratore*; a collection of speeches excerpted from Sallust's *Bella* and *Historiae*; and fragments of Quintilian (Reynolds and Wilson 1968: 82–88). The survival of rhetoric in the Middle Ages, however, was not limited to the transmission of classical rhetorical treatises; rhetoric also drew strength from the production of new works.

During this age of educational reforms, the seven liberal arts were divided into two curricula: the *trivium*, consisting of grammar, rhetoric and dialectic, and the *quadrivium*, consisting of arithmetic, geometry, astronomy and music. Under this system of education, the schools—which were attached to the monasteries and cathedrals by imperial edict—flourished. Intellectual centers such as Tours, Fleury, Auxerre, Lorsch, Reichenau and St. Gall not only preserved classical rhetorical treatises but also produced handbooks on rhetoric. The principal example of these rhetorical handbooks came from Alcuin himself, when, in 796, he adapted the *De Inventione* of Cicero and Julius Victor's *Ars Rhetorica* to produce his famous treatise, *The Rhetoric of Alcuin & Charlemagne* (Howell). These handbooks, in monastic and cathedral libraries and schools, conclusively prove that rhetoric had survived and was now established within the educational structure of the *trivium* and *quadrivium*. Thus, as the educational institutions evolved and expanded from monastic and cathedral centers into universities by the twelfth and thirteenth centuries, the heritage of rhetoric became more deeply embedded and preserved within the educational system.

Conclusion

Greek rhetoric in the late Roman Empire and into the Middle Ages is a study of severance and restraint under tumultuous social conditions. Rhetoric had gained widespread popularity in the Roman Republic because of its utility as a tool of political power. It had survived the transformation from Republic to Empire because it was the central focus of the educational system. Rhetoric had further survived the challenge of the absolutism of Christianity because wise Church fathers such as St. Augustine recognized the persuasive and educational value of a transformed Christian rhetoric. Rhetoric had managed to survive the barbarian invasions primarily because it was lauded by the schools of Gaul, which desperately clung to it as the symbol of the last vestiges of the Roman Empire. At a time when rhetoric all but disappeared from the Continent, it was preserved by English and Irish scholars such as Alcuin who eventually helped promote a Carolingian renaissance under the patronage of Charlemagne. Secured as an established part of the educational system, rhetoric had found its place within the *trivium.* With the rise of universities and the Italian Renaissance of the fourteenth and fifteenth centuries, the preservation of rhetoric would be a certainty when Greek and Roman rhetoric were again reunited. In essence, rhetoric survived various phases of the Roman Empire and into the Middle Ages because it was perceived as a source of power—whether that power was political, educational, spiritual or cultural.

Conclusion
The Symbiotic Relationship of Greek Rhetoric and Roman Culture

The causes then, direct or contributory, to which the decay in the first century is assigned by our ancient theorists are the complexity of the Empire, degraded morality, debased education, general factors of cultural development (a natural "law" of reaction), and the loss of political liberty. The truth may well be that all these causes operated in a complex, but certainly the loss of political liberty is the major and ultimate consideration (Harry Caplan).

This book approached the study of Greek and Roman rhetoric through social interaction. In the past, broad categorical distinctions were made between Greek and Roman rhetoric. These portraits of distinct, contrasting features were understandable in the previous periods of humanistic research. Scholars enjoyed making bold and distinctive generalizations about the "glory that was Greece" and the "grandeur that was Rome." The modern, systematic study of the history of classical rhetoric—a process that is a little more than a century old—offers exciting new evidence which challenges previous assumptions. Our examination of Greek and Roman rhetoric shows an intertwined relationship. Understanding the relationship between Greek rhetoric and Roman rhetoric through cultural interaction helps us to better understand not only how rhetoric was shaped at Rome but also how rhetoric in turn shaped Roman culture.

115

One of the first and most important points made in this book was to illustrate the transmission and transition of Greek rhetoric to Rome. It is clear that Romans were exposed to Greek rhetoric directly from their contact with prominent mother cities such as Athens. It is now equally clear that Romans also learned much about Greek rhetoric indirectly through the Greek cities that began as colonies in Sicily and Magna Graecia. Roman exposure to and assimilation of these cities was reciprocal, for the testimony of Greek influence ranging from the dialects of Southern Italy to the Hellenic rhetoric itself is well articulated by several early Romans. Despite some resistance, the value and benefits of Greek rhetoric far outweighed the conservative desire for preserving the pristine virtues of Roman culture and the Latin language. Greek rhetoric was introduced and assimilated into Roman society by exposures which ranged from household tutors to imperially supported sophists.

Schools of declamation were integral components in the social environment of Rome. So influential were these schools that previous portrayals of them as glib and derivative must now be dismissed as inaccurate. Scholars such as S. F. Bonner and D. A. Russell, in their respective treatments of Roman and Greek declamation, have emphasized how sophisticated and pervasive the study of declamation was. We have reviewed the important place declamation had as the vehicle for transmitting Greek rhetoric and for "Latinizing" Greek rhetoric for Romans. The sustained popularity of schools of declamation, the number of prestigious Romans who benefited from the educational experience, and its endurance are all indices of its cultural impact.

It is also clear that rhetoric survived the Roman revolution from Republic to Empire because rhetoric was able to make a transition from a political tool to an educational value. In this respect we see also how Greek sophists helped in this transformation by establishing a standard of education that would make Athens the educational center of the Roman Empire. This transformation also altered the relationship of Greek rhetoric with Romans. The importance of patronage emerged as the single most important element in the perpetuation of Greek rhetoric in the Roman Empire. The study of this patronage is apparent in two respects: first, the support of imperial and municipal chairs of rhetoric and cultural building programs in cities such as Athens; second, the Roman support of oratorical and literary performances throughout her Empire, as illustrated by the discussion of the Amphiareion of Oropus.

While Greek rhetoric contributed to the evolution of Roman rhetoric, it also continued its own development under Roman rule.

Changes took place as Roman authority shifted from a Republic to an Empire, but changes in the connection between orality and literacy also occurred. Systems of Greek rhetoric contributed both to effective speaking and to the rise of Roman literary art. In the early stages of the Empire, particularly under the Augustan Principate, literary artists such as Virgil, Horace and Livy used their writing skills to make artistically rhetorical statements about culture. In a similar respect, Greek rhetoric shifted away from the more politically expedient forms of discursive practices to those *technai* that stressed the finer stylistic points of oral and written performance. These changes, as argued here, are best understood as a manifestation of *letteraturizzazione*—the appropriation of features of primary, orally agonistic rhetoric that facilitate the aesthetic features of both literacy and oratory modeled on the stylistic principles of literary impression.

The final chapter of this book provides an overview highlighting those historical events which illustrate the consequences of the severance of Greek rhetoric from the Latin-speaking West. The consequences of this severance—brought about not because of intellectual reasons but because of social and political forces—altered the study of rhetoric for the rest of its history. Roman rhetoric was restricted in the West to the Ciceronian tradition with only those connections to Greek rhetoric inherent in his works. Similarly, Greece, which had never chosen to reciprocate in the assimilation of Roman rhetoric into her culture, turned inward to her own heritage and built on that tradition in the growth of Byzantine rhetoric.

For almost a millennium, the separation of Greek rhetoric from Roman culture persisted. For historians of rhetoric the "renaissance" began when the West discovered her own long-lost ancient authors and eagerly received the Greek scholars who fled to Europe with the fall of Constantinople in 1453. It is important here to mention, and perhaps fitting to conclude, that this re-assimilation of Greek rhetoric and Roman culture returned a vitality to the study of rhetoric that had not been present for centuries. So interested were Westerners in re-discovering the Hellenic origins of their discipline that the subsequent attention to rhetoric enhanced the historical scholarship of the period and provided the milieu to contribute much to the advancement of new or modern versions of rhetoric. In this respect, the renaissance of Greek rhetoric in the West is akin to our own present-day experience of re-discovering how a more sensitive accounting of the history of rhetoric can inform us of new, important perspectives on current understanding of the discipline.

Works Consulted

Primary Sources

All classical works cited are listed by their classical title and referenced by their standardized citation numbers. Oxford or Teubner editions are recognized as the best editions of classical texts in their primary language, while translations for many of the classical texts cited here are available in the Loeb Classical Library Series of the Harvard University Press. All translations, unless otherwise stated, were done by the author.

Aelius Aristides. *On Rome.*
_____. *Panathenaikos.*
_____. *The Sacred Tales.*
Aeschylus. *Septem Contra Thebas.*
Apollodorus Mythographus. *Bibliotheca.*
Appian. *The Civil Wars.*
Archaeologihe Ephermeris (1885), 3; (1923), 41; (1925), 43.
Aristotle. *Ethica Nicomachea.*
_____. *Rhetoric.*
Athenaeus. *Dipnosophistae.*
_____. *The Sacred Teachings.*
(St.) Augustine. *Confessions.*
_____. *De Doctrina Christiana.*
Aulus Gellius. *Noctes Atticae.*
Cicero, Marcus Tullius. *Brutus.*
_____. *De Amicitia.*
_____. *De Finibus.*

Cicero, Marcus Tullius. *De Lege Agraria.*

_____. *De Legibus.*

_____. *De Natura Deorum.*

_____. *De Officiis.*

_____. *De Oratore.*

_____. *De Inventione.*

_____. *De Natura Deorum.*

_____. *De Oratore.*

_____. *De Officiis.*

_____. *De Optimo Genere Oratorum.*

_____. *De Republica.*

_____. *Epistulae ad Atticum.*

_____. *Epistulae ad Familares.*

_____. *Epistulae ad Quintum Fratrem.*

_____. *In Catilinam.*

_____. *In Verrem.*

_____. *Orationes Philippicae.*

_____. *Orator.*

_____. *Paradoxa Stoicorum.*

_____. *Partitiones Oratoriae.*

_____. *Post Reditum in Senatu.*

_____. *Pro Archia Poeta.*

_____. *Pro Balbo.*

_____. *Pro Ligario.*

_____. *Pro Marcello.*

_____. *Pro Rege Deiotaro.*

_____. *Pro Roscio Amerino.*

_____. *Tusculanae Disputationes.*

Cicero, Quintus. *Commentariolum Petitionis.*

Diodorus Siculus.

Diogenes Laertius.

Eunapius. *Vitae Sophistarum.*

Ennius. *Varia.*

Hieronymus. *Chronica: Ab Abraham.*

Hyperides. "Speech in Defense of Euxenippus."

Inscriptiones Atticae: Euclidis Anno Anteriores.

Inscriptiones Graecae 3.

Inscriptiones Graecae: Megaridis, Oropiae, Boeotiae 7.

Livy. *Ab Urbe Condita.*

Lucian. *Eunuchus.*

Malcovate, Henrica, ed. (1953). *Oratorvm Romanorvm Fragmenta: Liberae Rei Pvblicae. I: Textvs.* Torino: G. B. Paravia & Co.

Pausanias. *Description of Greece: Attica.*

Petronius. *Satyricon.*

Philodemus. *Rhetorica.*

Philostratus. *Vitae Sophistarum.*

Plato. *Euthydemus*.

_____. *Gorgias*.

_____. *Ion*.

_____. *Leges*.

Pliny (the Younger). *Epistulae*.

_____. *Panegyricus*.

Plutarch. *Vitae Parallelae: Cato Maior*.

_____. *Vitae Parallelae: Cato Minor*.

_____. *Vitae Parallelae: Cicero*.

_____. *Vitae Parallelae: Lucullus*.

_____. *Vitae Parallelae: Pericles*.

Polybius.

Quintilian. *Institutio Oratoria*.

[   ]. *Rhetorica ad Herennium*.

The Rhetoric of Alcuin & Charlemagne (1965). Trans. Wilbur Samuel
    Howell. New York: Russell & Russell.

Scriptores Historiae Augustae.

Seneca (the Elder). *Controversiae et Suasoriae*.

Seneca the Younger. *De Tranquillitate Animi*.

Strabo. *Geography*.

Suetonius. *De Grammaticis et De Rhetoribus*.

_____. *De Viris Illustribus: Divus Augustus*.

_____. *De Viris Illustribus: Domitianus*.

_____. *De Viris Illustribus: Gaius Caligula*.

_____. *De Viris Illustribus: Divus Iulius*.

_____. *De Viris Illustribus: Nero*.

_____. *De Viris Illustribus: Otho*.

_____. *De Viris Illustribus: Divus Vespasianus*.

Supplementum Epigraphicum Graecum.

Tacitus. *Dialogus De Oratoribus*.

_____. *Germania*.

Tertullian. *De Anima*.

Thucydides. *The Peloponnesian War*.

Valerius Maximus. *Memorable Deeds and Sayings*.

Xenophon. *Memorabilia*.

_____. *The Polity of the Athenians*.

Secondary Sources

Adkins, A. W. H. (1973). "*Arete, Techne*, Democracy and Sophists:
    Protagoras 316b–328d." *Journal of Hellenic Studies*, 93: 3–12.

Ancient Greek and Roman Rhetoricians: A Biographical Dictionary
    (1968). Ed. Donald C. Bryant et al. Columbia MO: Artcraft Press.

The Athenian Agora (1990). Fourth ed. Princeton, NJ: American School
    of Classical Studies at Athens.

Avontins, I. (1975). "The Holders of the Chairs of Rhetoric at Athens."
    Harvard Studies in Classical Philology, 79: 313–24.

Baldwin, Charles Sears (1959). *Medieval Rhetoric and Poetic to 1400: Interpreted from Representative Works.* Gloucester MA: Peter Smith.

Behr, Charles Allison (1968). *Aelius Aristides and the Sacred Tales.* Amsterdam: Adolf M. Hakkert.

Bitzer, Lloyd F. (1968). "The Rhetorical Situation." *Philosophy and Rhetoric,* 1: 1–14.

Boardman, John (1964). *The Greeks Overseas.* Baltimore: Penguin Books.

Bonner, Stanley F. (1977). *Education in Ancient Rome: From the Elder Cato to the Younger Pliny.* Berkeley and Los Angeles: University of California Press.

_____ (1969). *Roman Declamation in the Late Republic and Early Empire.* Liverpool: Liverpool University Press.

Bourne, Frank C. (1966). *A History of the Romans.* Boston: D. C. Heath.

Bowersock, G. W. (1966). *Greek Sophists in the Roman Empire.* Oxford: Clarendon Press.

Brackman, A. (1974). *The Dream of Troy.* New York: Mason & Lipscomb.

Bryant, Donald C. (1965). "Rhetoric: Its Function and Its Scope." The *Province of Rhetoric.* Eds. Joseph Schwartz and John A. Rycenga. New York: The Ronald Press: 3–36. Reprinted from the *Quarterly Journal of Speech,* December 1953.

Caplan, Harry (1970). "The Decay of Eloquence at Rome in the First Century." *Of Eloquence: Studies in Ancient and Medieval Rhetoric.* Eds. Anne King and Helen North. Ithaca and London: Cornell University Press, pp. 160–95.

Carcopino, Jerome (1970). *Daily Life in Ancient Rome.* Ed. Henry T. Rowell. Trans. E. O. Lorimer. New Haven: Yale University Press.

Ceram, C. W. (1972). *Gods, Graves, and Scholars: The Story of Archaeology.* Second ed. Trans. E. B. Garside & Sophie Wilkins. New York: Bantam Books.

Clark, Donald Lemen (1966). *Rhetoric in Greco-Roman Education.* New York: Columbia University Press.

Clarke, M. L. (1971). *Higher Education in the Ancient World.* London: Routledge & Kegan Paul.

_____ (1966). *Rhetoric at Rome: A Historical Survey.* London: Cohen and West, Ltd.

Conley, Thomas (1990). *Rhetoric in the European Tradition.* New York and London: Longman.

Curtius, Ernst Robert (1963). *European Literature and the Latin Middle Ages.* Trans. William R. Trask. New York: Harper Torchbooks.

D'Alton, J. F. (1962). *Roman Literary Theory and Criticism.* New York: Russell & Russell.

Deuel, L. (1977). *Memoirs of Heinrich Schliemann: A Documentary Portrait Drawn from His Autobiographical Writings, Letters and Excavation Reports.* New York: Harper & Row.

Duff, J. Wright. (1964). *A Literary History of Rome in the the Silver Age: From Tiberius to Hadrian.* Ed. A. M. Duff. Third Edition. London: Ernest Benn Limited.

Dunbabin, T. J. (1948; 1989) *The Western Greeks.* Oxford: Clarendon Press (reprint, Chicago: Ares).

Ehrenberg, Victor (1948). "The Foundation of Thurii." *American Journal of Philology,* 69: 149–70.

Enos, Richard Leo. (1979). "Epigraphical Sources for the History of Hellenic Rhetoric." *Rhetoric Society Quarterly,* 9: 169–76.

_____ (1993). *Greek Rhetoric Before Aristotle.* Prospect Heights IL: Waveland Press.

_____ (1988). *The Literate Mode of Cicero's Legal Rhetoric.* Carbondale and Edwardsville: Southern Illinois University Press.

_____ (1992). "Why Gorgias of Leontini Traveled to Athens: A Study of Recent Epigraphical Evidence." *Rhetoric Review,* 11: 1–15.

Enos, Richard Leo and John M. Ackerman (1991). "Walter J. Ong and the Archaeology of Orality and Literacy: A Theoretical Model for Historical Rhetoric." *Media, Consciousness, and Culture: Explorations of Walter Ong's Thought.* Eds. Bruce E. Gronbeck, Thomas J. Farrell, and Paul A. Soukup. Newbury Park CA: Sage Publications.

Enos, Richard Leo and Karen Rossi Schnakenberg (1994). " Cicero Latinizes Hellenic *Ethos." Ethos: New Essays in Rhetorical and Critical Theory.* Eds. James S. Baumlin and Tita French Baumlin. Dallas: Southern Methodist University Press.

Freeman, Edward A. (1892). *The History of Sicily.* Volume III. Oxford: Clarendon Press.

Gibbon, Edward (1845). *The Decline and Fall of the Roman Empire.* Five volumes. Philadelphia: Porter & Coates.

Gold, Barbara K. (1987). *Literary Patronage in Greece and Rome.* Chapel Hill and London: The University of North Carolina Press.

Goody, Jack and Ian Watt (1988). "The Consequences of Literacy." *Perspectives on Literacy.* Eds. Eugene R. Kintgen, Barry M. Kroll, and Mike Rose. Carbondale: Southern Illinois University Press, pp. 3–27.

Graham, A. J. (1983). *Colony and Mother City in Ancient Greece.* Second edition. Chicago: Ares.

Gwynn, Aubrey (1926). *Roman Education from Cicero to Quintilian.* Oxford: Oxford University Press.

Haarhoff, Theodore J. (1920). *Schools of Gaul: A Study of Pagan and Christian Education in the Last Century of the Western Empire.* London: Oxford University Press.

Havelock, Eric A. (1982). *The Literate Revolution in Greece and Its Cultural Consequences.* Princeton: Princeton University Press.

Howell, Wilbur Samuel (1965). *The Rhetoric of Alcuin & Charlemagne: A Translation, with an Introduction, the Latin Text, and Notes.* New York: Russell & Russell.

Hoyt, Robert S. (1966). *Europe in the Middle Ages.* Second edition. New York: Harcourt Brace & World.

Kinneavy, James L. (1986). "*Kairos:* A Neglected Concept in Classical Rhetoric." *Rhetoric and Praxis: The Contributions of Classical*

Rhetoric to Practical Reasoning. Ed. Jean Dietz Moss. Washington, D.C.: The Catholic University of America Press.

Kennedy, George (1963). *The Art of Persuasion in Greece.* Princeton: Princeton University Press.

_____ (1972). *The Art of Rhetoric in the Roman World: 300 B.C.–A.D. 300.* Princeton: Princeton University Press.

_____ (1983). *Greek Rhetoric Under Christian Emperors.* Princeton: Princeton University Press.

_____. (1980). "Later Greek Philosophy and Rhetoric." *Philosophy and Rhetoric,* 13: 181–197.

_____ (1975). "Review Article: The Present State of the Study of Ancient Rhetoric." *Classical Philology,* 70: 278–82.

Lesky, Albin (1966). *A History of Greek Literature.* Trans. James Willis and Cornelis de Heer. Second ed. New York: Thomas Y. Crowell Company.

Lofberg, John Oscar (1976). *Sycophancy in Athens.* Chicago: Ares.

Lot, Ferdinand (1931). *The End of the Ancient World and the Beginnings of the Middle Ages.* Trans. Philio Leon and Mariette Leon. New York: A. A. Knopf.

Lundy, Susan Ruth and Wayne N. Thompson (1980). "Pliny, A Neglected Roman Rhetorician." *Quarterly Journal of Speech,* 66: 407–17.

MacKendrick, Paul (1960). *The Mute Stones Speak: The Story of Archaeology in Italy.* New York: Mentor.

Marrou, H. I. (1956). *A History of Education in Antiquity.* Trans. George Lamb. New York: Sheed and Ward.

McDonald, A. (1943). *The Political Meeting Places of the Greeks.* Baltimore: The Johns Hopkins Press.

Merritt, Benjamin D. (1947). "Greek Inscriptions." *Hesperia,* 16: 147–83 (esp. 170–72).

_____ (1966). *Inscriptions from the Athenian Agora.* Princeton, NJ: American School of Classical Studies at Athens.

Murphy, James J. (1965). "Rhetoric in Fourteenth-Century Oxford." *Medium Aevum,* 34: 1–20.

_____ (1974). *Rhetoric in the Middle Ages: A History of Rhetorical Theory from St. Augustine to the Renaissance.* Berkeley: University of California Press.

Nicholson, Reynold A. (1956). *A Literary History of the Arabs.* Cambridge: Univeristy Press.

Ochs, Donovan J. (1993). *Consolatory Rhetoric: Grief, Symbol, and Ritual in the Greco-Roman Era.* Columbia: University of South Carolina Press.

Perlman, S. (1963). "The Politicians in the Athenian Democracy of the Fourth Century B.C." *Athenaeum,* 41: 327–55.

Petracos, Basil C. (1974). *The Amphiareion of Oropos.* Athens: Esperos Editions.

Poulakos, John (1990). "Interpreting the Sophistical Rhetoric: A Response to Schiappa. "*Philosophy and Rhetoric,* 23: 218–28.

Reynolds, L. D. and N. G. Wilson (1968). *Scribes and Scholars: A Guide to the Transmission of Greek and Latin Literature.* London: Oxford University Press.

Rhodes, P. J. (1972). *The Athenian Boule.* Oxford: Clarendon Press.

Roberts, W. Rhys (1904). "The New Rhetorical Fragments (*Oxyrhynchus Papyri*, part III., pp. 27–30) in Relation to the Sicilian Rhetoric of Corax and Tisias." *Classical Review,* 18: 18–21.

Russell, D. A. (1983). *Greek Declamation.* Cambridge: Cambridge University Press.

Schiappa, Edward. (1990). "History and Neo-Sophistic Criticism: A Reply to Poulakos." *Philosophy and Rhetoric,* 23: 307–15.

———. (1991). *Protagoras and Logos: A Study of Greek Philosophy and Rhetoric.* Columbia: University of Southern Carolina Press.

Scullard, H. H. (1963). *From the Gracchi to Nero: A History of Rome from 133 B.C.—A.D. 68.* London: Methuen & Co. Ltd.

Sealey, Raphael (1976). *A History of the Greek City States: 700–338 B.C.* Berkeley: University of California Press.

Shear, T. Leslie (1935). "The Campaign of 1933." *Hesperia,* 4: 330–34.

——— (1936). "The Campaign of 1935." *Hesperia,* 5: 1–42 (esp. 41–42 [I2729] and suppl. 8, 268–72).

Sihler, E. G. (1914). *Cicero of Arpinum.* New Haven: Yale University Press.

Sochatoff, A. Fred (1939). "Basic Rhetorical Theories of the Elder Seneca." *Classical Journal,* 34: 345–54.

Sullivan, Richard E. (1960). *Heirs of the Roman Empire.* Ithaca NJ: Cornell Univeristy Press.

Syme. Ronald (1963). *The Roman Revolution.* Oxford: Oxford University Press.

Taylor, Lily Ross (1968). *Party Politics in the Age of Caesar.* Berkeley and Los Angeles: University of California Press.

Thompson, Homer A. (1950). "The Odeion in the Athenian Agora." *Hesperia,* 19: 31–141.

Vanderpool, Eugene (1949)."The Route of Pausanias in the Athenian Agora." *Hesperia,* 18: 128–37.

Walden, John W. H. (1970). *The Universities of Ancient Greece.* Freeport, NY: Books for Libraries Press.

Wilcox, Stanley (1942). "The Scope of Early Rhetorical Instruction." *Harvard Studies in Classical Philology,* 53: 121–55.

Woodhead, A. G. (1962). *The Greeks in the West.* New York: Frederick A. Praeger Publisher.

Wooten, Cecil W. (1973). "The Ambassador's Speech: A Particularly Hellenistic Genre of Oratory." *Quarterly Journal of Speech,* 59: 209–12.

———, trans. (1987). *Hermogenes' On Types of Style.* Chapel Hill and London: The Univeristy of North Carolina Press.

Index